THE ULTIMATE PLAYBOOK FOR HIGH ACHIEVEMENT:

11 Keys for Success in Sport and Life

D0110275

Alex Molden

Shark Effect
PUBLISHING

The Ultimate Playbook for High Achievement:

11 Keys for Success in Sport & Life

Alex Molden

Copyright © 2021 | Alex Molden

Disclaimer

This book is for educational purposes only. The views expressed are those of the author alone. The reader is responsible for his or her own actions. Adherence to all applicable laws and regulations, including international, federal, state, and local governing professional licensing, business practices, advertising, and all other aspects of doing business in the United States, Canada, or any other jurisdiction is the sole responsibility of the purchaser or reader. Neither the author nor the publisher assumes any responsibility or liability whatsoever on the behalf of the purchaser or reader of these materials.

DEDICATION

— ◇ —

To Christin, my beautiful wife and best friend, thank you for helping me write this book. Isaiah, Elijah, Micah, Alana, Selah, Josiah, Bianca, and Ezra. You are all my inspiration and the reason I started my journey to improve myself and become more intentional in my words, actions, relationships, and thoughts.

To my mom (Cassandra Lewis), pops (Alvin Molden), my twin brother (Lenar) and all the coaches, trainers, Nike managers, and teammates of mine throughout the years. Thank you for pushing me to see myself as someone who is more than an athlete.

To: Athletic Directors, Directors of Player Development, Coaches, Parents & Athletes

My name is Alex Molden, and I'm an inspirational speaker and personal development coach who helps individuals prepare to succeed in any environment. I've spoken at Fortune 500 companies, leadership seminars, personal development retreats, and on college campuses—I'd be honored to speak at yours!

My passion stems from my sports background (NCAA Football All-America, 1st round draft pick, 8-year NFL career), experience as a Nike Global Master Trainer, and my family (my wife and eight children). I understand the influence of student-athletes, and I know that if I can help them become better people, they will become better leaders in this world. Hip-hop culture and sports culture are two powerful influencers. Whether we like it or not, many of today's athletes either misuse their influence or ignore opportunities their impact can present.

This book, my keynote speeches, leadership workshops, and High Achievers Academy online course are all grounded in the feelings I experienced when I stopped playing football. When I retired from the NFL, I had no identity outside of my sport. Because I spent so many years believing that my ability, success, platform, and knowledge were my overall identity, I was frustrated. When my abilities started to fade and eventually, my platform since I was 12 years old was taken away from me, I didn't know who I was, and that was a terrible feeling. It's a reality that most people, not just athletes, must face if they haven't developed a strong sense of self. When people interact with me, I know exactly how I want them to feel when they leave our conversation: the feeling of empowerment that comes from knowing your identity. Please allow me the honor of empowering *your* athlete(s).

You can book a call with me or shoot me an email so we can schedule one. I look forward to serving you.

Alex Molden

Personal Development Coach | 1.800.818.2799 | info@alex.moldenspeaks.com | www.alexmoldenspeaks.com

CONTENTS

— ◆ —

PRAISE FOR ALEX AND THE HIGH ACHIEVERS ACADEMY

— ◆ —

"I've known Alex for many years and for as great as an athlete he is, he's a better person. Alex's life experiences as a high-level college athlete, NFL player, husband, and father give him a unique perspective on the challenges that face athletes. After a successful NFL career, he has done a remarkable job using the power of sports to transition from professional athlete to speaker and now author. One goal we should all have is to be around highly successful individuals who are passionate about their craft and want to help people. Alex checks all those boxes."

Mike Yam

NFL Network Anchor | Former Pac-12 Anchor

"Before I knew Alex as an 'inspirational speaker,' I knew him as a father of 8. I could tell by the way the family interacted and impacted others, they were under great leadership. I knew from that first interaction that he was someone that was making a great impact, not for the children in his home but everyone that came in contact with him."

Da'Vell Winters

Boise State University | Chief of Staff (Football)

"Alignment, Assignment, Adjustment, was a tool that Alex gave me to transition to the next chapter of my life during so much uncertainty. His positive mindset rubbed off on me and has helped me not fear what lies ahead. He's truly one of the best at what he does!!"

Ifo Ekpre-Olomu

NCAA Football 2x All-American

"What I think so many athletes struggle with is what to do when they aren't an athlete anymore. Just like Alex did and so many of us others have too. And that's why I love how this book speaks directly to that. We learn so much as athletes that can be directly applied to everything we do in life, and Alex has created the Playbook we can follow to do just that."

Patrick Curran

Co-Founder | Curran Media

"Alex Molden is the epitome of learning and leadership. His ability to connect, motivate and inspire others, specifically student-athletes is remarkable. Although his accomplishments as an athlete and professional are elite, it is his heart for growth in his own life and the lives of others that make him world-class."

Henry Barrera

Liberty University | Men's Basketball Director of Performance

"If you are ready to achieve success as a student athlete, this book is a must read to be high achieving. Through his amazing experiences, Alex Molden, shares how to navigate the challenges facing you today and provides the best methods he used to become one of the most elite athletes in the country. You were created to be an achiever, and this book is your roadmap to success."

Doug Hix

Director of Development | Coram Deo Academy

"Alex has taken everything he learned as a professional athlete, trainer, and coach and applied it to both life and the business world in the way we lead, connect, collaborate and thrive. His ability to mentor and motivate has been invaluable to me throughout my personal career and also helped in bringing my teams closer together."

Morgan Shaw Parker

VP/Chief Marketing Officer at AMB Sports & Entertainment (Atlanta Falcons & Atlanta United MLS)

"Everyone agreed that Alex was the highlight of our two-day retreat. I would love for his full-day workshop to be the first of many that Alex comes out and does for my team. I'd love for us to continue to build on the rapport we have established with Alex and further enable my team to grow."

Megan Radonich

Converse | Senior Director of Finance

"Absolutely fantastic! One of the best speakers I have ever heard! Honored to have him share his wisdom with the team today. Alex took learning and insights from an American sport and made them relevant in business and life for a global audience. Alex was simply legendary for our team."

Kieran Ronan

Nike | Global Equipment GM

"Our team walked away from his talk with a newfound sense of excitement to take on our competition and Alex provided us with the tools to do so. I can truly say we are all Built to Win after his talk."

Ali Houlihan | Hiya | Office Manager

"Alex is one of the most caring people I know. Since our playing days with the San Diego Chargers, he's always tried to help people be the best version of themselves."

Curtis Conway

NFL Veteran WR (12 years) | NFL, NCAA Football Analyst

"I've had the opportunity to benefit from what Alex brings to the table from both a personal standpoint and from an outside observer standpoint and both have been inspiring. Alex not only pours into those he comes in contact with but he also does an amazing job of listening/learning from others in a way that he's then able to apply another level of support and motivation. If you're looking for lasting

impact that extends into multiple facets of your life, Alex is someone to have on your team."

Astor Chambers

Beats by Dre | Global Influence & Social Actions Lead

"Alex Molden's professional development talk is genuinely one of inspiration and admiration. He truly is an admirable and authentic speaker who leans into his talks to help many see the true value of what he conveys to be the best version of themselves in their career journey."

Ebony (Travis) Tichenor, MBA

Boston Scientific | Global HR Director

"In his inspiring book, 'The Ultimate Playbook for High Achievement: 11 Keys for Success in Sport & Life,' former NFL star, motivator, leader, and an all-around inspiring human, Alex Molden, empowers student-athletes to be successful, impactful, and purposeful when transitioning to the real world. Speaking from real-life experience, the scars, tragedies, and ultimately his many triumphs, Alex and 'The Ultimate Playbook for High Achievement' are powerful guides for athletes to be significant, impactful, and successful both on the field and, ultimately, in the real world."

Tommy Breedlove

Wall Street Journal and USA Today | Best-Selling Author of the Book *Legendary*

"In Alex Molden you will see an authentic person wanting the reader/listener to believe in themselves and turn life experiences into motivation. Each iteration of the concepts put forth by Alex are realistic, achievable and measurable."

Reggie Jordan

Assistant Athletic Director at the University of Central Oklahoma

CHAPTER 1:

LAYING THE FOUNDATION FOR WHO
YOU WANT TO BE

— ◇ —

When my second-oldest son was recruited to play football, I told him to listen closely to what the coaches sell. They would all sound great. The campuses and facilities would be out of this world. And yet, *he* was ultimately responsible for determining what his foundational "cornerstones" would be. Academics, playtime, coaching, culture, relationships, conference, bowl games, whatever: *You*, the student-athlete, must be the one to figure this out.

We visited USC, Stanford, the University of Oregon, and the University of Washington. Other schools that offered him scholarships were Utah, LSU, Colorado, and Notre Dame, to name a few. Each team tried to sell him/us on why their university was the right fit for him and his skills, but the one university that stood out from the others was the University of Washington. Why, exactly? Due to the simple fact that they believed developing the leader within their athletes was more critical than honing their athletic skills.

Coach Chris Petersen developed the team's leadership program called "Built for Life," aimed at cultivating student leadership skills that would ultimately spread into other aspects of their life after their athletic careers concluded.

"When they're really good at life and the life skills that go with it, their football is usually really good as well," Petersen said. "When their life isn't in order, they struggle on the football field."

After reading this quote in a news article, I cast my vote for the University of Washington (despite in fact hating the school, as a University of Oregon alum). UW's words and actions showed they sought to develop their athletes into men and women who would not just identify as athletes, but also understand who they *are* beyond what they *do*.

Looking back at my career, I would have loved to go through a program like this. Whether in college, the NFL, or even after I was done playing, these concepts would have served me well in any environment.

Whether you're a weekend warrior, armchair quarterback, elite athlete, parent of an athlete, aspiring athlete, or even a struggling athlete, I believe, just like Nike says in its ads, "If you have a body, you are an athlete." And as such, we can all improve on how to influence others and gain more awareness of how *we* are influenced. It is crucial that we understand how our natural, God-given gifts can also hurt us if we lack the character to see ourselves outside the platform of athletics. In doing this, we become better leaders. It starts with recognizing that we are more than just athletes.

Here are the key steps:

- Align your words, actions, values, and motives with your foundation.

- Assign who you want to be and the character you will need to have.

- Adjust your relationships, how you view yourself, and how you want to be viewed.

- Assess the decisions and outcomes of those decisions to help you become the high-achieving person you dream of, both within and outside of your sport.

These are all fundamental keys that will help any athlete [1]become the high achiever he or she is meant to be.

IS THE PERSON YOU <u>DON'T</u> WANT TO BE DESCRIBED BELOW?

-De'Anthony was a freak of an athlete and high school hoop phenom. He received a full-ride scholarship to play at his dream school. De'Anthony burst on the scene as a baller with tremendous upside. Unfortunately, during his sophomore campaign, he suffered a fracture in his lower back that eventually ended his hoop dreams. He was angry, frustrated, and above all else, sad. His plan of playing in the NBA and

---

1   Athlete – If you have a body, you are an athlete (Nike motto)

supporting his mom immediately vanished!

Due to his lack of discipline when his circumstances changed (he stopped going to class, missed numerous engagements with his academic advisor, and skipped rehab appointments), he dropped out of college. De'Anthony was homeless for a couple of months and eventually found a job as a janitor at his old high school.

- Sam was a recent graduate of Bucknell University. As a student-athlete on the football team, he received pretty good grades and played great on the field even though he needed to learn a whole new defensive system his senior year. Now, Sam works in construction on the East Coast. He deals with conflict daily and struggles to connect and communicate with his coworkers. Sam misses the game and camaraderie he enjoyed in college. He feels as though he's participating in someone else's purpose, not his own. He acknowledges he is lucky to have a job, but feels drastically unfulfilled, unmotivated, and uninspired.

- Samantha was a successful softball player who had played the game for well over ten years by the time she got to college. Her family had invested thousands of dollars in clinics, camps, private coaching, physical therapy, and speed and strength training. She had a successful career at the collegiate level. Samantha was offered plenty of internship and alumni mentoring opportunities, but she never took advantage of these chances for enhanced self-growth. As a 30-year-old single mom, she now regrets this. Samantha watches former teammates enjoy great success in their personal and professional lives because they took advantage of opportunities her college offered with respect to internships, alumni mixers, resume building workshops, and job shadowing.

I share these stories to help you see the big picture of this book's intentions: to inspire you to view your life experiences as a means to propel you into a world of new relationships — on and off the field/court/diamond/mat—that can help you in your role as an entrepreneur, salesperson, coach, businessman/woman. At the root of all of this is necessary self-discovery: unearthing your purpose in life, your passion(s), and what character changes are needed for you to become the best and most intentional influencer you can be.

YOU ARE PUSHED OR PULLED TO BECOME THE BEST VERSION OF YOURSELF

You're either pushed or pulled to use your experiences, knowledge, and even your failures to propel you past your limits to do or create something unique.

In 2001, I signed a lucrative contract offer to play with the San Diego Chargers. I was excited to enjoy a new beginning in a much better climate after spending my first five years in hot and sticky New Orleans! But how did I end up there? On the first day of free agency, the San Diego Chargers called. I was in the middle of a round of golf with a couple buddies at our local country club. It was a beautiful 70-degree morning with only a few clouds dotting the sky. Ahead on the front nine, I heard my phone start to ring. I answered and was thrilled to learn it was John Butler, general manager of the San Diego Chargers, on the other end of the line.

"Alex, how would you like to be a San Diego Charger?" I was beyond excited! One, they called me on the first day of free agency — which made me feel like they really needed me — and two, I would get a chance to live on the West Coast, closer to my wife's family and mine too.

After flying out to San Diego and participating in interviews with the entire Chargers organization, the team offered me a 6-year contract worth 16 million dollars. My agent, wife, and I agreed to the contract terms, and I was officially a Charger.

During my first San Diego minicamp, I tore my meniscus while covering a receiver during very competitive 1-on-1 drills. When this happened, I didn't really think too much about it, but the continued swelling did concern me a bit. I rehabbed it and strengthened the surrounding muscle groups, but my knee wasn't the same as it was pre-injury. Before our first game, I got a Toradol shot, which made me feel amazing. I went on to play one of the best games of my career. Due to swelling and pain I experienced afterwards, I underwent the first of two surgeries that year with the Chargers. My season was cut short, and I was placed on IR (Injured Reserve).

During spring the following year, the Chargers threw a "draft-day party" at Qualcomm Stadium, where fans got a chance to meet and interact with their favorite players. The sun was beaming, and the sky was as blue as our powder blue uniforms. Hotdogs, popcorn, kids' bounce houses, autograph sessions, and pictures galore completed the scene. The stadium's big screen showed the draft on ESPN, which was held in New York City. Although I used to watch the draft religiously in previous years, I hadn't been that concerned with doing so ever since the Saints drafted me back in 1996. As a child, I remember sitting on our living room couch watching college superstars such as Deion Sanders, Barry Sanders, Derrick Thomas, and Steve Atwater walking up to the commissioner and taking pictures, their jerseys proudly boasting the number one. I would imagine myself in their shoes — though at the time I was only a bony kid from Colorado Springs. But on that day in Qualcomm Stadium, I heard NFL Commissioner Paul Tagliabue suddenly announce, "With the 5th pick in the 2002 NFL Draft, the San Diego Chargers select (long pause)...Quinton Jammer, Cornerback (University of Texas)." My heart sank into my stomach. *I* played cornerback! The other starting cornerback on the team was Ryan McNeil, who was selected to the pro bowl the previous year. After the shock wore off and I was on my way back home, I understood why they drafted Quinton. My two surgeries the prior year had left the team feeling insecure and potentially depleted at the cornerback position; they had to find a way to ensure adequate depth and athleticism for their defensive backs, plus there were still concerns about my knee AND ankle.

In turn, I had expected a call from John Butler or my agent, telling me the Chargers were ending my contract. But my phone never rang. I continued training with the team during our off-season program but felt anxious the entire time. I assumed everyone in the building knew I would get released from my contract as soon as Quinton signed his.

When we reported to training camp in late July, I was very nervous, as you might expect. I'd seen dudes get "cut" as soon as they checked in. I had my suitcase, fan, pillow, and other things to make the next couple of weeks feel as close to home as possible. After I checked in and received my dorm keys (our training camp was held at the University of San Diego), I heard, "Alex, when you get settled in your room, I need for you to come to see me" — a request from John Butler. My heart dropped! I'd never been "released" before, but at that moment, I felt so embarrassed and helpless because my future was in someone else's hands.

I knocked on John's door, and he said, "Alex? Come on in, have a seat." I felt like a lamb led to slaughter. "Alex, we're going to restructure your contract." I had ZERO leverage because I had only played in a handful of games the previous year. "We're going to pay you the minimum," which meant $550,000 (the veteran minimum); I had been scheduled to make $2,100,000 that year!! However, he then told me that if I played 65% of the defensive snaps, I would get a $387,000 bonus; 75%, another $387,000 bonus; 85%, another $387,000; and 95%, I would receive a bonus check of $1,550,000, so all of my money "back" (in one check)! Without checking with my agent, I quickly said, "Where do I sign?"

You see, I knew what it would take to stay on the field and play well even with a small shark (Quinton Jammer) now in my fish tank. We had a brand-new coaching staff, which meant we had to learn a whole new defensive scheme and new terminology. However, the fact that I had my own personal system already in place gave me a sense of calm despite the circumstances.

This system, which I will explain in depth later on in subsequent chapters, can provide a sense of stability: Alignment, Assignment, Adjustment, and Assessment. Because of my attention to detail across these four key areas, I ended up having the best year of my career. Notice I didn't say anything about my athleticism, which had very little to do with it. It was no secret that I had slowed down because of my injuries, but the AAAA system helped me play at a much faster level than I had in previous years. Oh, and I *did* receive all of my money back...in one lump sum!

The bottom line is that I was forced to refocus my game.

When the Chargers drafted Quinton, that situation brought me back to my foundation. I refocused, which allowed me to enjoy the best year of my career.

The four afore-mentioned pillars also led to success off the field. It took me some time to figure out exactly how I could use these principles to help when I retired from my sport, but after some deep soul searching and with support from others, I developed these four keys (along with seven more) to help one become a high achiever.

COACHING QUESTIONS FOR HIGH ACHIEVERS:

- What pushes or pulls you to achieve your goals?

- Do you have a system in place that keeps you on track?

- Do you believe you have a God-given gift? If so, what is it?

- Do you believe your character will allow that gift to not negatively impact your persona? (It takes a strong person to not let success and resulting relationships exert an undesirable influence)

- What gives you a sense of stability?

CHAPTER 2:

LEADERSHIP:

WHAT IT IS AND HOW TO USE IT EFFECTIVELY

— ◆ —

"If you can't explain it to a six year old, you don't
understand it yourself."
-Albert Einstein

When I tried to figure out the game of football as a kid, I couldn't ask my dad because he never watched or played it. The Internet wasn't around in the early '80s. I was too embarrassed to ask some of my buddies how the game is played, so I had to do the next best thing: crack open an encyclopedia. Those pages provided me with foundational information required to understand the positions, formations, offensive and defensive terminology, and player responsibilities. I was then able to understand football at the granular level. This foundational knowledge gave me so much confidence. After reading this chapter, you will understand the foundation of leadership and its impact on every part of your life.

We often get this notion of leadership confused with character traits or how people "show up" or their work ethic. This definition is not valid! When you boil it down to its core, leadership is *influenced*: nothing more, nothing less. Allow me to explain...

I'd like to share something that I learned from my life coach, Eldridge Broussard: the ten influencers of leadership. Based on these ten things, you will understand how to recognize when someone is trying to influence you. Know that there is nothing wrong with that, but there IS something wrong when you fail to realize this is happening. You will also be able to use these ten pillars to influence others, predict others' behavior, and employ better decision-making skills.

These are in no particular order; *you* can decide which ones are most important and how to align them with your life.

Character

Who you are (Integrity; moral principle, honest, upright, and sincere)

What character should you create to find success? What is it that keeps you up at night—that thing you can't wait to do the following day? Now, ask yourself this question: What kind of character is needed for you to do that particular thing? Does it align with your core values and beliefs? Have you performed the personal research needed to find out who you are? For example, stepping on stage to give a speech takes a tremendous amount of confidence, boldness, and vital self-knowledge. If you're shy, lack confidence when you speak, and have not researched your material, you will—put bluntly—suck! You must start to take on the burden of first personally knowing if you will be a successful speaker, no matter the topic.

It works both ways, too. Let's say you set out to be the best garbage collector in the world. What type of character is needed for you to reach that goal? Would you need to be ruthless, intelligent, cunning, business-savvy, good decision maker, keen eye, considerate, team-oriented? I think most of these character traits would fit quite well if being the best garbage collector in the world was the overarching goal. The key takeaway is: Are you able to sustain the character required to get you where you want to be?

Ability

What you can do (*Power to do something physical or mental; skill, expertise, or talent*)

Ability can open up doors for you, no doubt. Your ability to run fast, jump high, react quickly, or be accurate can persuade people to give you a chance, or even a second chance, to join a team. Think of other abilities you possess that could be helpful outside of your sport:-engaging with people-reading body language-finishing tasks-being creative-taking feedback/coaching wellThese are all abilities that most people have a

13

difficult time doing. Hopefully, as you grow and get older, you will start to develop your abilities across varied areas.

Knowledge

What you know (*Facts, information, and skills acquired through experience or education: the theoretical or practical understanding of a subject*)

In some instances, it's all about the knowledge you have. Many people spend so much time, energy, and money trying to grow their understanding of finances, history, mathematics, and science while spending little to no time gaining knowledge about themselves. They never really sit down and ask themselves questions like: Who am I? What am I passionate about? What do I hate most? Who do I want to help the most? What drives me?

Success

What you have achieved (*Accomplishment of a goal or purpose*)

Typically, we believe this pillar of leadership means more than the others, which is in fact true sometimes. But we have to *research* our success by asking ourselves some simple questions like:

- How did I find success in this situation?

- Was there a specific environment that helped me

(stressful or stress-free, chaotic or controlled)?

- Was there someone who helped me or hindered me when I found success?

- How can I duplicate this success?

We tend to look at success as a good thing, but did you know that it can alienate you from others? How often do you love hearing about others' success beyond that of your children or significant other? There is an appropriate time and place for you to "brag" on you. The most effective way for you to share your success is when others in fact do so, whether you're present or not. This situation arises all the time. When you're with a friend who introduces you to another friend you don't know, pay attention; does he or she lead with what you do, your success, or both? This will show exactly how your friend views you and what's most important to him/her. Act with intention when it comes to how others view your success!

Failure

What you did not achieve (The omission of expected or required action)

Due to negative connotations associated with failing at something, most people don't consider this an influencer. Rather, we try to sweep it under the proverbial rug. Yet, when you can own up to your mistakes and take ownership of the mishaps or roadblocks you failed to see or even created, this will do wonders for you. The reason why, you ask? It makes you more relatable to others.

Ask yourself these questions:

- Which personal mistakes, once you owned up to them, made you look even better than before the error occurred?

- Is there a person you admire who made an error in judgment, and once he or she took ownership of it (no matter how difficult), seemed to become more likable?

Here's the thing: We all make mistakes, and when we do, it's best to own up to them and use them as a teaching tool for ourselves and others. In the world of sports, specifically, consider some athletes who made well-publicized mistakes and went on to learn from their experience (Kobe Bryant, Tiger Woods, Sammy Sosa, Mark McGwire, Michael Irvin, Conor McGregor, Ray Lewis, etc.).

Platform

What you do (*a raised level*)

What you do, your job, your social media footprint, your status are all considered a platform. For young people, this often exists as a leading influencer. Think about this. Kim Kardashian had very little influence before her famous

Ray J sex tape came to light. However, her mom used this seemingly negative incident as an opportunity to grow her (and her family's) platform. Kim's beauty, hit show *Keeping up with the Kardashians*, and marriages went on to grow her overall influence. The cool thing is, she now shows us just how intentional she is with her platform by using it for good (e.g., bringing awareness to the US justice system's unfair treatment of African-Americans) in addition to purely monetary gains.

Experience

Where you have been (The knowledge or skill acquired by experience over a period of time, especially through working in a specific profession)

Experience is tricky. Too much emphasis is often placed on this. And to be honest, way too many people overvalue it!

Consider a coach who has been with a program for over 30 years, but he or she has never won a league/conference title or championship. Would you want to learn from them or hire them as a coach for your team? Don't get me wrong; I believe experience is good. Still, we need to dive into what type of experience is needed for a particular job or task. How important is the "right" kind of experience for you? People with a specific skill set or character might be great for a particular job but are passed over due to a lack of experience. High school and college graduates, former pro athletes, former military officers, and former convicts may lack expertise. Still, they have other abilities and knowledge that could be a huge benefit to others.

Intuition

How you feel (The ability to understand something immediately, without the need for conscious reasoning)

This pillar of leadership is the most powerful, but it is also the most unstable of all the influencers. How you make people feel can pull them toward you or push them away from you.

When I was a performance training tech during my years at Nike, I would often share the set with many high-profile athletes. Most would barely pay you any attention if you didn't play a specific role relevant to them and the shoot. It was just the norm. One encounter that stuck out to me was when I assisted on a photo shoot with Nike and Roger Federer. He made it a point to say hello and shake everyone's hand on set! It didn't matter if you were in lighting, makeup, equipment, or security; he made sure to introduce himself and thank us for being there and doing our jobs. He made us feel seen and valued! I'm not a big tennis guy, but that day I became a huge Roger Federer fan.

In interacting with other people, Federer was intentional in how he wanted to make them feel. By the same token, *everyone* should be aware of their words and actions towards others and what underlying things or manipulation could be happening at that moment. As a dad and high school football coach, I set out to make my kids and athletes feel empowered and confident when they are not with me. So, I let them know when they are doing something correctly by ensuring everyone is aware: by screaming, hollering, and jumping up and down. When I need to correct them, I do so calmly, often asking questions about the situation and what they saw. I also put my hand on their shoulder or give them a side hug. I want them to know that even though I'm correcting them, I'm not judging who they *are*. I'm just simply correcting their *actions* and trying to understand their intentions.

Communication

How you share (*The imparting or exchanging of information or news*)

There are five different ways of communicating:

1. Verbal – Conversation and storytelling

2. Written – Letters, email, social media

3. Oral – Videoconferencing, talking; depends on speed, volume, pitch, voice modulation, clarity of speech

4. Non-Verbal – Reading what is between the lines in written communication and hearing the unsaid in verbal communication

5. Physical Communication – Body language

It's essential to understand how you communicate

your thoughts and ideas. They can be interpreted in several different ways. You must master the art of communication, and it's not all about how you do so verbally. Think about how you share. Be aware of how people will receive the information you're injecting into the world. Think before you speak and/or press send!

Are you aware of your tone when you speak to others? Not everyone you interact with understands your sense of humor. Rolling your eyes or clucking your tongue when you're talking to someone can make them feel a certain way. Are you aware of it? Do you look into the eyes of the people with whom you speak? It says something about you when you don't: that you're not trustworthy, lack confidence, and/ or have something to hide.

Relationships

Who you know (A connection, association, or involvement)

Relationships you currently have or want to create are key facets of leadership. As parents, we must now know the relationships our kids are engaged in. My mom didn't know the relationships that my brother or I had. She wasn't exposed to the character of my friends. Conversely, my wife and I make it a point to know possible influences in our kids' lives and who they in turn may influence.

It is essential to realize that the people you know will

influence others in some way. It helps to do research before you forge relationships with people. Because if you don't, you might be found guilty by association should something go awry. Be mindful of the relationships you build, which can either bring you down or lift you up emotionally and psychologically.

Nevertheless, the most important relationship you should have is the one you share with yourself. Are you comfortable being who you are or the person you set out to be? Do you truly know yourself (strengths, weaknesses, flaws, shortcomings, etc.)? Ask yourself these questions out loud if you have to!

In summary, understanding these ten influencers can help you make better decisions and prioritize both how you want to be influenced and influence people in return. Try to remember someone from your "past life" who influenced you – good or bad – there is no judgment here. To what extent did he/she affect you?

For example:

a) My defensive backs coach, Willie Shaw (23 years)

b) My good friend and high school teammate, Brian, aka "Lumpy" (4 years).

What were the top influencers that inspired me to follow them? (Platform, success, failure, character, communication, relationships, knowledge, intuition, ability, experience)

Willie Shaw

1. Experience
2. Knowledge
3. Success
4. Ability
5. Character

6. Platform
7. Communication
8. Intuition
9. Relationships
10. Failure

Lumpy

1. Platform
2. Success
3. Relationships
4. Knowledge
5. Experience

6. Failure
7. Character
8. Intuition
9. Communication
10. Ability

HIGH ACHIEVER COACHING QUESTIONS:

- How do you want to influence people (your friends, children, spouse/significant other, employees, etc.)?

- How does each one rank, from most important to least important, for you?

- Do you want to influence people around you? If so, how?

CHAPTER 3:

ALIGNMENT

—— ◇ ——

When it comes to setting and achieving goals, you need to align your thoughts, actions, relationships, and character accordingly. Whether you're trying to land a job, find a boyfriend or girlfriend, adopt a healthier lifestyle, or win the starting position on your sports team, you must align yourself with the qualities required to attain whatever you set out to achieve.

At each level of my football career, I had a coach. My high school coach taught me foundational skills and drills. My college coach(es) taught me concepts. My first NFL defensive backs coach, Jim Mora Jr., taught me a ton of drills—but very few of those drills directly applied to the actual game. I ultimately wanted a system of success that was predictable and dependable. Then God placed Coach Shaw in my life!

Willie Shaw became my coach when Mike Ditka took the reins of the New Orleans Saints in 1997. Willie had served as both a defensive backs coach and defensive coordinator at the pro and collegiate level since the 1980s. His knowledge of both offense and defense was unmatched, and to say that I was excited to learn from him is an understatement.

My first meeting with Coach Shaw came during our spring minicamp. He was a wiry gentleman in his early 60s who had bags under his eyes (most likely from many sleepless nights spent watching hours of game tape, I'm sure) and gray hair. After one practice, Coach Shaw yelled to me, "Hey 2-5, come over here for a second!" I was intrigued but also nervous. I jogged over, and he said, "You want to know the secret for success in this league?"

"Oh, yes, sir!" I replied. I anxiously anticipated what I assumed would come out of his mouth: a verbal map to a treasure chest filled with diamonds, gold, silver, and pearls.

Instead, he uttered just three words: "Alignment. Assignment. Adjustment."

I thought to myself, *That's it? That's the secret to success as a professional football player? There's got to be more to it than that! Study 40 hours a week to learn an opponent's weaknesses and strengths...maintain 4% body fat...run a 4.40 forty-yard dash... give me something more, coach!*

"2-5," Willie said, "Until you can line up correctly and have the proper alignment for every coverage and call we make, you won't be able to make the plays you're supposed to make. In fact, if you're not aligned correctly, you'll get beat before the play even starts."

I'd never really heard the importance of alignment like that before.

"You gotta know your assignment (inside and out), but not just that. You have to know the assignment of your teammates. Every one of them."

Okay, I thought. *This is new.*

"As for adjustment, you must be ready to adjust before, during, and after the play. This means you need to know the playbook inside and out, forward and backward. When you can do this, you have a system that you can depend on."

With this new knowledge under my belt, it still didn't feel like I had the holy grail of football success just yet. However, I did start to pay attention and be more intentional in how I studied game tape and, more importantly, practiced.

Slowly, this high-speed and complicated game started to slow down for me and the complexities of various offenses became more straightforward. I began to make more plays in practice, boosting my confidence, and with that confidence, made more plays when they counted — in the games!

When I spent some time coaching one of my personal development clients who had recently graduated from college, one of the first things we talked about was his struggle to adjust to life after sports. He had enjoyed a fantastic career playing football at the Division I level. Still, he became frustrated at the lack of guidance he received in college about job skills or training to find a career that best fit his knowledge and personality. Our conversation went a little something like this: "Are you done blaming others?" He replied, "What?" I continued, "Did you have personal development counselors or leadership directors at the facility?" Visibly frustrated, he replied, "Ummm yeah. They used to send us articles about interview skills and leadership stuff." I said, "Well, there you have it. You didn't see the opportunities that were right in front of your face. The first thing needed to set your path toward personal development is to not only discover a career that fulfills you, but take responsibility for everything that happens or happened to you in the past. But even before that, you need to learn how to lead yourself."

I began to ask him questions about the things that gave him enjoyment. After that, I inquired about things he was good at. I then asked him about what he thought was lacking in society, overall. In my final question, I asked him to name a point in his life that inspired him to become the best version of himself, in or out of sports.

After answering all of these questions, he determined that becoming a middle school teacher and coaching high school football would be the most rewarding career path. He said, "Alex, you made me realize that I can make an impact on someone like that younger me, a knucklehead with no guidance and no apparent future outside of sports. I know how to help influence these kids." I asked, "And how's that?" He replied, "I can help them see that all the adversity they have faced can actually be the best thing that ever happened to them. I can share *my* experiences and the experiences of others, showing how we adapted and changed for the better."

I told him, "Think deeper. The most impactful thing you said was that you want to HELP people like the younger you! You are on the right path to find fulfillment in your life."

Another aspect of alignment is obtaining "buy-in" from everybody involved. When my coach told us why we aligned "8x1" (8 yards off the WR and 1 yard inside or outside), I understood we were trying to take something away from the opponent (leverage-wise). This alignment creates a little bit of separation to get our "reads and keys" to anticipate the route or route combinations and make quick and intelligent decisions based on meaningful information. When told the "Why" of our alignment, I became more deeply rooted in our defense, the coach, and what my purpose was.

About eight months after retiring from the game I loved, life was pretty stagnant. I took the kids to school, walked the dogs, and played a ton of golf, but other than that, it felt like I was just floating around. I was a "Ronin," a samurai with no master. I soon became friends with one of my neighbors, the CEO of a very successful nonprofit agency in Carlsbad, CA. She asked me if I would ever consider coming to work for her part-time as a development consultant. I needed meaning in my life and thought that joining a nonprofit would lead to meaningful work, so I jumped at the chance to get out of the house and learn something new. I was only there for six months, but I learned a ton in the process (writing grants, event planning, securing donations, writing reports, etc.).

Because of some intel we had about the housing market in California, my wife and I decided to move to Portland, Oregon in the summer of 2006. We figured it was a wise move (literally and figuratively!) since we didn't have any real roots (family, career, networks) in San Diego. We assumed our NFL money would last longer in the great Northwest. My wife's family was in Portland. I would have more business opportunities because of my playing career at the University of Oregon and in the NFL. A couple months after moving up to Portland, I began looking for job opportunities in the nonprofit sector. A few weeks into my search, I found a desirable management position. I applied for the role and ended up getting an interview. In my mind, I assumed I was a shoo-in. I had experience in the nonprofit world. I was a former professional athlete. I had graduated from the University of Oregon. I enjoyed name recognition in the area. And finally, I'm Black (which in the Northwest made me a super minority). I prepared for the interview in the same way I used to prepare for football games — memorizing everything I needed to know — in this case, the organization's mission statement, clients served, history, specific events, etc. On the day of the interview, I was so prepared I considered the process a mere formality. In my mind, I was beyond the perfect candidate. I wasn't concerned about the pay either; in fact, the NFL donated $5,000 to any nonprofit organization that employed a former player on a full-time basis!

As I got up and engaged in my regular morning routine

(showering, brushing my teeth, doing some mobility exercises, and getting dressed), I started getting butterflies in my stomach. I hadn't had that feeling in a while, when I used to experience it coming out of the tunnel and running out onto the field before games: smoke blasting from the fog machines, cheerleaders, teammates slapping you on your butt and helmet, the dazzling light show, Ozzy Osbourne's "Crazy Train" intro blaring, and the announcer saying, "At cornerback, coming out of the University of Oregon....Alex Molden!" All these things would release anyone's butterflies from their own internal chrysalis. However, during my last year in the NFL with both the Washington Redskins (now the Washington Football Team) and Detroit Lions, I had zero butterflies. I've thought about this for a while, and I think the reason is because I had gotten released and cut twice in an 8-month timeframe. Being told you're not good enough and lacking confidence in your abilities can sap any feelings of excitement.

"Good afternoon, Mr. Molden. Please have a seat; Mrs. Tulane will be with you shortly," said the lady at the front desk. I hadn't been that nervous since my meeting with Mike Ditka when I had asked to be traded almost ten years prior. The door swung open, and a small, light-skinned Black lady in her late 50s, who seemed just as sweet as apple pie said, "Mr. Molden, I'm ready for you now."

I confidently leaped to my feet and walked into her office.

"So, Mr. Molden, tell me what you know about our organization," she said.

I answered her questions about the organization and the people they served almost perfectly.

She asked, "Do you know why we do what we do?"

There was a long awkward pause.

"Do you know our purpose?"

Again, awkwardness.

She then asked me one of the simplest yet most profound questions I've ever heard in my life, "Do you know *your* purpose, Alex?"

"I don't," I responded.

"Why do you even want this job?" After a couple of seconds that felt like an eternity, I said, "I just need to get out of the house and start a new career."

She looked at me the way I envision my son's first-grade teacher would look at him if he misspelled a word like "the" or "can." "

What is your passion?" "

I don't really know," I said.

She leaned back in her chair and said, "Alex, can I give you a bit of advice?"

I nodded, holding back tears.

"Before you go on any more job interviews, I suggest you

find out exactly who you are because right now, it seems that football was who you *were*, but now that's gone." She stood up, opened her office door, and offered a polite, "Good luck to you, darlin'."

I walked to my car, got in, and cried my eyes out.

After banging my hands on the steering wheel, I composed myself and firmly decided I never wanted to feel this way again. I'd been released, cut, let go, and fired from jobs before, and it was embarrassing; the long walk to your locker and bagging up your stuff under the watchful eyes of team security is no fun. In fact, it's awkward as hell—but I would much rather do that than endure this scenario again!

YOUR FOUNDATION

We discussed how important it is to align your life, but what do you align your life *with*, exactly? What's the foundation? A strong foundation, just like that of a well-built house, can withstand adversity (strong winds, earthquakes, thunderstorms, etc.). Perhaps for you, adversity presents itself as sickness (we're in the midst of a global pandemic right now), economic downturn, or wrongful incarceration: These can all rock you to your core as things you possibly have no control over. But what if you in fact consciously make decisions that negatively affect you? Things like gambling and going into debt, being unfaithful to your significant other, making bad decisions because of emotions, entering into an ill-advised relationship, etc. In any of these cases, your foundation should do three things:

1. Provide you with support when adversity happens

2. Give you peace of mind when making decisions

3. Help you make the best decision possible

Many of my clients come to me because they feel stuck and realize that how they experience life is based on feelings or intuition. As we discussed in the previous chapter, this is the most unstable way to make decisions. The foundation can change day to day or conversation to conversation. The bottom line is, when you afford certain people or situations in your life a "two-way go" (a football term giving receivers the option to release to either side of a defender), standards or guardrails must exist in your life to protect you from pitfalls and setbacks.

During one session with my life coach Eldridge, he asked me to put these in order based on their importance to me at that time (2016):

- Family

- Career

- Faith (where values tend to live)

- Hobbies

- Health

I said, "Family, career, faith, health, hobbies."

This session took place amidst one of my best fiscal years (outside of football), during which I traveled worldwide to train high-profile athletes. Despite the monetary gains, my relationship with my wife was shaky at best, and I wasn't emotionally present for my kids. I felt like a success but found it difficult to look in the mirror and actually say it. Deep down, I knew this wasn't sustainable, nor what I wanted my marriage to be.

And so, there was a long pause (maybe a minute or so) before I just broke down crying. I told Eldridge, "I know this isn't right. I know my faith should come first."

He simply asked, "Why?" and then, "Where in the Bible makes you believe that not putting your faith in God first will cause you not to prosper?"

In actuality, prioritizing my faith helped me see that God will never change despite other circumstances that might come up along the way. On top of that, it made me see the importance of having a solid relationship with Him, first and foremost. This would ultimately amplify my family and how I valued them as part of my life. Since that conversation with my coach, my life has not only been more peaceful but more intentional overall. I see my actual value in this world and how I can impact it in a positive manner.

We *all* bring value to this world. The problem is that most of us are not intentional in finding it, owning it, and sharing it!

For any athletes (at any level) reading this, I'm here to tell you that despite popular beliefs, your value on this Earth is not how fast or quick you are. Shoot, it's not even how good-looking you are—or think you are! Rather, remember that your value comes from understanding who you are and then sharing that light with the world—but only if that light can help others!

TOOLS TO ALIGN YOUR VALUES

To identify your values, I want you to write down 6-10 values that are important to you (e.g., kindness, wealth, family, faith, friends, career, hobbies, etc.). Next, rank them in order from most to least significant. Now, spend 5-10 minutes writing down why you ranked them the way you did. The fourth thing I want you to do is write down how you "practice" these values on a day-to-day basis. Finally, write down anything you might do on a daily basis that could work against these values. Examine your values, one by one. This exercise is not intended to make you feel bad or guilty: it is to simply identify if you are in or out of alignment with who you want to be.

When I perform this exercise, it is eye-opening to see how often I am out of alignment with who I want to be. This is basically a splash of cold water to the face, seeing if your words align with your actions.

HIGH ACHIEVER COACHING QUESTIONS:

- Are you consistently aligned to your values?

- Do you have a passion? Do you have a purpose in your life?

- What is a non-negotiable for you when it comes to making decisions?

- Do you know who you are?-What are some things you can do every day to align yourself at work and home?

CHAPTER 4:

ASSIGNMENT

— ◇ —

What's your big goal when you finish school?

What's your big goal when you finish playing sports?

What are the positives and negatives of attaining it?

How will that make you feel?

By attaining this goal, what will it do for you?

What type of character will you need to adopt to achieve this?

These are all questions I never asked myself when I finished college and my career as a professional athlete. If only I had done so, I would have saved myself so much emotional pain and suffering. I would have found my passion sooner and been more intentional in leveraging my platform and influence.

I recently took my 12 and 19-year-old sons to a basketball tournament out in Pocatello, Idaho. While there, I had a chance to visit with one of my old high school teammates. While staying with him, I ended up befriending one of the most prominent dairy farmers in Idaho. He wanted to give us a tour of his dairy farm, and I begrudgingly took him up on his offer.

Turns out, I was blown away by the sheer magnitude of this farm and the efficiency with which it was operated.

First off, the farm was massive. I mean, over 100 acres (22 of which are climate-controlled).

- 24,000 cows

- Each cow is worth $1,000-90 employees

- 3 nutritionists

- Each cow produces 84lbs of milk/day (milked for 12 mins. twice/day)

- 780,000 pounds of milk/day

- 40 calves born/day-50lbs of poop per cow/day-At 14 months of age, cows are bred

- If cows produce less than 40 lbs. of milk per day, they are turned into beef!

-$60 million/year in revenue!

The biggest takeaway I had was this: Cows are creatures of habit. They eat at a specific time. They go to their same milking station. They get milked at a particular time, and they go to sleep at a particular time.

They don't have any feelings. They must produce. They

have an assignment and a purpose in life (no matter how they feel about it).

It doesn't matter if you're a former collegiate athlete, professional athlete, coach, real estate agent, sales broker, product line manager, customer service rep, entrepreneur, or a cow. It's all about knowing your role and producing accordingly.

As an NFL player, knowing your assignment is the most basic and essential thing you need to know. It didn't matter how high you were drafted, how much money you make, where you fall within the depth chart, or what type of relationship you share with the coaches or front office staff. You need to know your job and role on the team.

However, if you want to have success and a long career, you must know not only your role but the roles of those around you. On every play, it's essential to understand your assignment and players who could positively or negatively affect the outcome. When I learned this, it provided a "big-picture" view of the meaning behind my team's position. I also learned who I could and could not trust when playing. For so many years in high school and college, I felt alone on the football field. If I just did my job, that was good enough; and if my teammates did their job — boom — we would win.

During my rookie NFL year, I learned a ton of defensive coverages. I already knew some from college, but the depth of knowledge and execution of each one was mind-blowing.

In college, we played a "Cover 4" scheme, in which each defensive back was responsible for a fourth of the field. In the "league," we played a "match-up zone" Cover 4, which meant we had to read our keys based on the receiver's route and combination of *multiple* receiver routes. The scheme could transform from zone to man-to-man in the blink of an eye.

In training camp, I learned the nickel position, reflecting a more undersized, quicker linebacker role. My job was to jam up the inside receiver and take the first person to the "flat" area (from the line of scrimmage to 10-15 yards along the field's perimeter). Seems pretty simple, right?

In our first preseason game, we played against the New York Giants. As we approached the two-minute warning in the second half, the Giants had the ball and were driving on us. We played a lot of man-to-man in this particular game. Towards the back half of the 4th Quarter, we started playing Cover 4 (I later learned this was the best fit). On first down, I jammed the receiver and then covered the running back to the flat (Herschel Walker!!).

"Don't let him inside!" our starting free safety (Greg Jackson) yelled to our linebackers. During the next play, the same thing happened. I jammed the receiver and "sat" in my zone, waiting to carry my next threat.

"Hey Rook, stop fucking letting him inside!" Well, this time I knew exactly who he was talking to. During the two-minute warning, Greg slapped me in the back of the helmet (in front of 70,000 fans), yelling, "Rook, stop letting him inside! When you do that, it puts a ton of pressure on me, and when there is pressure on me, I can't help EA (Eric Allen-our All-Pro corner) on the post route."

I didn't know that! My coach had just told me to "jam" the receiver and take the first threat to the flat. Now, Greg was feeding me specific information about his job and how I can help him better perform in his role. After the timeout, I made it a point to not only jam the receiver but to do so inside-out to help the guys behind me. Lo and behold, EA intercepted the ball on that very next play because of how I changed my approach.

Knowing your role can help you understand the big picture for many things.

Knowing your role as an individual is very important as well. Finding your purpose in life can be one of the most rewarding, yet most challenging, things you undergo. It takes a real time investment and what I call "self-scouting." And here's the thing: Your purpose doesn't always stay the same. Just like how I needed to know different coverages and roles as an NFL defensive back, there will be times when *your* purpose changes.

For many years, I thought my purpose was to play football. My character (who I was) was intertwined with my ability and my platform, and when I stopped playing, it felt like I was lost, like I had no purpose. I had a degree in psychology, millions of dollars in the bank, nice cars, multiple homes, a beautiful family, but I felt empty, depressed, and worthless. After meeting with Mrs. Tulane (as discussed earlier), I began searching out who I was while seeking to learn my purpose.

My friend Tommy Breedlove is a *Wall Street Journal* and *USA Today* bestselling author. He's an Atlanta-based business owner and relationship and mindset coach who is regularly featured as a keynote speaker at global events. Tommy launched his 20-year corporate career at one of the largest financial consulting firms in the world. Eventually, he became a shareholder in and international practice leader/member of the board of directors for one of the largest public accounting and financial firms in the southeastern U.S. At the height of his career, Tommy experienced a transformational moment that inspired him to walk away from the corporate world to change his life and follow his purpose.

Tommy says there are three things you must do to lay the framework for finding your purpose:

1. Choose to do something different

2. Invest in yourself

3. Take continued action

Both an art and a science, finding your purpose reflects the intersection of these three steps:

Step 1) Finding your God-given talents or "superpowers." If you don't know what these are, seek out the five people you spend the most time with and they will tell you.Step 2) Ensuring you love engaging in that talent or that superpower. Step 3) Learning what the world needs or what you despise in the world.

It took some time to figure this out for myself, but I merely applied what had helped me in my football environment. Self-scouting was something we did after every four games, wherein we would watch game tape of ourselves and then write down our tendencies. Good, bad, or indifferent, you had to look at the film, and what you saw was the truth — your "on the field" character was always on display.

After "self-scouting" myself, I realized I had a gift for simplifying otherwise complex movement patterns in the training world. I also learned that I could connect with people. I loved training and working with young athletes who wanted to achieve great things in their respective sports. I also knew the world needed better, more influential trainers to shape young athletes to become better on and off the field. At the center of it all, I just wanted to *help* people.

As I studied leadership principles and began applying them to my own life, I realized how powerful this gift truly was: It can help people become better humans.

Coaching Points

- Write down 15-20 things you enjoy doing
- Write down 1-10 things for which you have a specific skill set

- Write down 5-10 things the world needs more of, in your opinion

HIGH ACHIEVER COACHING QUESTIONS:

- What are some things you can't stand in life?

- What are some things you can do to improve that (within your network, knowledge, or experience)?

- What are some of your strengths? If you don't know, ask a couple people you are close to.

- What are some of your limitations right now? Ask if you don't know or haven't pinpointed them yet.

CHAPTER 5:

ADJUSTMENT

— ◇ —

One of the most significant adjustments I ever had to make was adjusting to life after sport. Doing something I loved since I was 12 years old and then abruptly stopping at the ripe age of 32 was hard: missing the early-morning practices I used to love (and at the same time, hate), long lines at the training table to get taped up, the smell of fresh-cut grass, the cheering (and the booing), traveling with my coaches and teammates while getting to know them at a deeper level, and of course—the paychecks! But the biggest thing I had to overcome was the lack of a daily schedule.

Workouts, meetings, practices, travel, eating, classes, massages, chiropractors; you name it, and it was on a schedule. That schedule provided a sense of comfort, a sense of efficiency and accountability, which allowed me to focus on being the best athlete and teammate I could be.

In my post-NFL life, it took me a while to figure out that I thrived on having a schedule. I began writing out a plan for my week the day or night before. Things like working out, taking the kids to school, cleaning the house, doing chores, and running errands for my wife all became my new job. I knew I needed more. I needed to find my purpose and my "new" passion. I had to adjust how I saw myself, as well. I was more than a former NFL football player.

YOU ARE THE FIRST LINE OF DEFENSE

It didn't help that people still viewed me as exactly *that* (a former NFL baller). I knew that was the case because whenever I was introduced to someone's friend, neighbor, or colleague, that person would say, "Meet my good friend Alex...he played in the NFL." I had to start reframing how people saw me, while still acknowledging my unique role as an elite athlete and former pro football player. I tailored my introduction accordingly by tacking on "...but now I am a stay-at-home dad" or "...but now I am a personal development coach." As athletes or former athletes, we are the first line of defense in educating others that sports are just what we *do/did*, not who we *are*. Even in relationships you've had for most or all of your life, it's never too late to reframe how people see you. Another way to do this is through your actions. It's one thing to tell people you're more than an athlete and another to show it. Researching other interests you might have (golf, surfing, networking, traveling, etc.) will serve you well, shining a light on you without needing to utter a word.

Kobe Bryant, before his untimely death, was very interested in several things: things like writing, soccer, and expanding the WNBA. He was more than a basketball player. He researched himself and unearthed things outside of his own personal bball journey that interested him and gave him joy. On the other side of that coin, there is Delonte West. Delonte was the 24th overall pick in the 2004 NBA Draft by the Boston Celtics. He played with the Celtics and Cleveland Cavaliers, where he was teammates with LeBron James and reached the playoffs in each of his three years with the team before landing in Dallas. During the 2011 NBA lockout, the first-round pick applied for a job at a Home Depot and worked at a furniture store and Starbucks. The point guard's NBA career ended unceremoniously with the Texas Legends, the Mavs' D-League team, in 2015. It is said that Delonte had squandered over 50 million dollars and lived on the streets of North Texas and Maryland. He was also diagnosed with bipolar disorder in 2008, which must be taken into account.

I'm guessing, by Delonte's actions, that he never considered himself anything else but a basketball player.

Now I know that as elite athletes, you must maintain a laser-beam focus on your sport while taking care of your body. Still, I believe you can do even more by taking care of your mind, expanding it and asking yourself questions about...yourself. Questions like:

- What do I like doing outside of my sport?

- What do I love doing outside of my sport?

- What else am I good at?

- How do I want to impact the world besides providing entertainment while playing my sport?

ADJUSTING YOUR RELATIONSHIPS

Think about your relationships that might be primed for adjustment. Do they help or hinder you from reaching your goals and aspirations? Some relationships that make you feel comfortable and relaxed during times of acute focus can be bad for you. Others that cause discomfort can in fact be the best thing for you.

One of my coaching clients revealed that the relationship she valued the most while in college was the one she shared with her strength and conditioning coach. She had played basketball at a Division I university on the East Coast and said, "From day one, this strength coach made us feel uncomfortable, not in a weird kind of way, but in a way that many of us never felt before. There was no smiling or joking around. It was serious, and many of us had never had a strength coach before entering college. Even when doing our movement assessments or our strength testing, we were required to do our best, and if we didn't, he would call us out in front of everybody!" I asked her if their relationship had changed as she got older and became more of a leader because of her experience. She replied, "Yes, it did. I ended up asking him why he was so harsh on incoming newcomers. He told me that many athletes who come into college have never really been pushed, and most have a sense of entitlement due to relentless praise from people (parents included) with respect to how fast, athletic, or accomplished they were in high school. This is the worst thing that can happen to college athletes." He wanted to ensure that every college athlete he coached felt like they were starting from ground zero. Their attitude, work ethic, and ability to help others were the only things praised on his watch: not winning or awards, but the journey.

When you play a team sport, you don't have a say in who coaches you. Hence, you are stuck trying to determine if the coach(es) have either your and/or your team's best interests at heart (quick spoiler alert—it's always the latter). You must shape your game around their coaching style. Yet, when you *do* have the opportunity to choose the relationships you want to engage in, you should ask yourself these questions:

- Do they make me a better person?
- Do they help me feel more confident?
- Do they hold me accountable for my words and actions?
- Do their words and actions align with my standards?
- Do they let their emotions or thoughts make decisions for them?

Before the 2001 season, I had just finished my contract with the New Orleans Saints, so I hit the free agent market.

As mentioned earlier, the San Diego Chargers was the first team to call. I leaped at the chance to don a Chargers uniform in sunny San Diego. I remember signing my contract, and the very next day, reported to the team's off-season training program. I was one of the only players there. As I was getting dressed, Junior Seau came strutting into the locker room. "Molden," he said, "Man, we sure are glad you're here." "You are a great fit for what we'll be doing defensively here... Glad you're a part of the team."

Junior Seau, a superstar NFL athlete, just told me he was glad I was there and that I would be an excellent fit for the team! I didn't know Junior at that time, but of course, I knew *of* him. Just hearing him say those words gave me confidence. I knew what I brought to the table in terms of my skill set, but hearing it from someone other than myself and management meant a lot. That moment in time helped me see how important it is for people who are established in a particular field, team, or environment to help others adjust by simply acknowledging them and sharing a few words of encouragement. Has anyone ever done this for you, or have you ever done this for someone new to your team, family, or neighborhood?

ADJUSTING YOUR CHARACTER

Your character is on display when you're in a position of power or at the pinnacle of your team, sport, or business. It is also on display when you make a mistake.

Justin Timberlake recently apologized to Britney Spears and Janet Jackson for benefiting "from a system that condones misogyny and racism" following backlash initially stemming from the release of the documentary *Framing Britney Spears*.

"The industry is flawed. It sets men, especially white men, up for success. As a man in a privileged position, I have to be vocal about this," Timberlake wrote in an Instagram post. "Because of my ignorance, I didn't recognize it for all that it was while it was happening in my own life, but I do not want to ever benefit from others being pulled down again."

Framing Britney Spears, which was produced by The New York Times and released in early 2021 on FX and Hulu, focused on Spears' tumultuous career. The documentary highlighted the fallout from Spears' breakup with Timberlake, in which Spears became a laughingstock while Timberlake's career continued to soar.

His apology sounds excellent and all, but it was long overdue! It shows he's trying to "put the fire out" now that the viral documentary is putting a spotlight on his past transgressions — and that he is only sorry his character, albeit from a long time ago, is being called into question.

JT is not the only person at the top of his or her game who shows character flaws. Superstar athletes such as Antonio Brown and Conor McGregor are two other examples. Once people started paying attention to how they treated others and their character started to outweigh their abilities, they felt the need to adjust who they were. Case in point, let's recap what

Antonio Brown did in the span of six infamous months during 2019:

- Demanded a trade from the Steelers

- Reported late to Raiders training camp (refusing to wear the league's new, safer helmets)

- Cussed out his boss (Raiders general manager)

- Accused of multiple counts of sexual assault and sexual misconduct

- Lied (on the record) to the Raiders head coach• Received battery charges for beating up his movers and damaging property

Based on Antonio's words and actions during his 2020-2021 NFL campaign that included a Super Bowl win with the Tampa Bay Bucs, he seemingly adjusted who he knew (insert future NFL Hall of Famer Tom Brady here) and built on that relationship to show he is indeed a "changed man." Just because you are quieter and out of the public eye doesn't mean you can't do this as well.

Mixed martial artist Conor McGregor saw his popularity start to spiral downward after he threw a chair and dolly at a bus in 2018, sending two other fighters to the hospital. He later turned himself in to authorities.

After this incident, Conor sought to change his ways and hired world-renowned life coach Tony Robbins to help him improve at taking ownership of his mistakes, changing his mindset, and finding authentic happiness. He became more aware of his emotions and how he allowed his feelings to guide his thinking. His past actions did not align with his current view of himself. He has since adjusted how he speaks to the media and treats his opponents (e.g., following his fight with Dustin Poirier, a battle lost, he pledged to donate $500,000 to Poirier's Good Fight Foundation).

Examine the times in your life that others (or even you) have told people they/you have changed. Words can be very influential, but actions are even more significant. How can you show that you've changed?

WHEN AND WHEN NOT TO ADJUST

My Oregon Ducks won the Pac-10 title in 1994, giving us a chance to play against the number one team in the country, the Penn State Nittany Lions. We started the year 1-2, but after a players-only meeting wherein we cleared the air, got on the same page, and started holding each other accountable, we finished out the season winning the next 7 out of 8 games and making it to the Rose Bowl for the first time in 37 years!!

We prepared for four weeks, studying Penn State's offensive strengths and weaknesses (they had very few). We knew we would need to play a near-perfect game as a team and especially as a defensive unit, which was our strength. We also learned we would need to "weather the storm" when things didn't go our way.

Right before our defense took the field, our defensive coordinator Nick Aliotti gathered us together. "What do you all think about running SMASH BLACK on the first play?" Smash Black was our all-out blitz. We were known as an aggressive defense that pressured the QB from different angles and at varied times in the game.

"Hell yeah!" we all said. We took the field on that bright and sunny day in front of 100,000 fans in Pasadena, California. "Smash Black, ready...BREAK!" We broke the huddle. Their top-ranked quarterback, Kerry Collins, easily avoided the blitz and handed the ball off to the best running back in the country (Ki-Jana Carter), who proceeded to trample one of our defensive backs, sprint 80 yards, and score a touchdown on the very...first...play!

Was there ever a time in your life when a leader, teacher, manager, or teammate decided to abruptly change an established plan based on a "gut" feeling? Earlier on in this book, I discussed how powerful intuition is an influencer. If you trust the data or information you have researched, you will more likely than not give yourself a better chance for success.

I learned a crucial lesson that day: Trust your preparation over fickle emotions. By calling a flashy blitz, our coach and

19-21-year-old defensive unit were influenced by the moment and the fans when we should have relied on our inherent preparation. We had never called "Smash Black" at the beginning of a game before, so why should we have done so in the biggest game of our careers to that point?

ADJUSTING OUT OF SPORT

The most significant piece of advice I can share is to start preparing earlier rather than later. Too many factors can arise in sports and derail your ambitions to play the game you love forever. Injury, coaching changes, scheme, age, politics involving younger, cheaper players who may have significant upside and are a better financial fit but lack experience: these are examples of factors that can all play a role in deciding to retire sooner than you'd like at the pro level. The same thing can happen to a collegiate athlete as well, minus salary cap politics.

The key is to start seeing yourself as more than an athlete, but rather, as someone who knows him or herself inside and out and can navigate inevitable situations for your benefit. It comes down to learning exactly what you want to do and become.

If you don't adjust, you can expect heartache and pain as you move through life, blaming others and feeling stuck, lost, and blind-sided because no one takes you seriously anymore.

When I speak to different college programs, I often talk

about adjustments that must be made before students leave college — adjustments about how they view themselves. Most student-athletes see themselves as athletes only, which is dangerous; their identity can get wrapped up into their sport and when they're done, they lose a huge piece of themselves in the process. When this happens, depression soon follows. The second critical element I cover is character adjustments that will most likely need to be addressed. As elite-level athletes, some things that fuel us and help us find success on the field can also hurt us away from it. Sometimes, our platforms as athletes and celebrities protect us from the realities of our character. After our talents diminish and our platforms fall away, we are left to address the truths of our character in new ways. Navigating this can be daunting, as many athletes are unaccustomed to facing negative effects from treating people poorly, engaging in transactional relationships instead of transparent ones, and lacking a mentor who can tell you the truth about how you show up in the world.

HIGH ACHIEVER COACHING QUESTIONS:

- How do you want to be remembered outside of your sport?

- What connections and/or networks can you become involved with while still playing your sport?

- Which character adjustments will you consider making as you transition out of your sport?

- Are there any environments you should consider adjusting to help you reach your goals and aspirations?

- Do you need to adjust the relationship you have with yourself and those close to you? (e.g., mom, dad, siblings?)

CHAPTER 6:

ASSESSMENT

— ◇ —

The ability to assess how you are doing is challenging but required when trying to improve on any aspect of your life. Fitness, athletic development, education, yearly or quarterly job performance reviews, and even personal development can and should be evaluated. Assessment is a tricky thing because it involves your ego, which you must learn to put in the backseat to reap the full benefits of this process.

Doc Rivers, a longtime NBA head coach and player, once said, "Average players want to be left alone, good players want to be coached, great players want to be told the truth."

Early on in my pro career, that was one of the biggest keys that helped me: the ability to be willing to hear the truth, not just to be coached. Coaching unlocks a person's potential to maximize performance, aiding the learning process. Opening that person's eyes to the truth hits a tad bit different. It gets at the foundation of what his or her words and actions say. Was there ever a time in your career when a coach told you the truth and it stung? What did you do with that information? Did you ignore it, or did you process it and use it to make you better? If shared by a reliable and unbiased source, that information is the key to improve yourself no matter the environment.

Towards the end of my career, I didn't want to be told the truth; I just wanted to be coached. The truth was; I had lost some abilities due to wear and tear from playing football for almost 20 years. Two ankle surgeries, three knee surgeries, and a sports hernia had slowed me down, and my coaches and teammates knew it. My ego impeded any chance for me to prolong my football career because I shunned advice about the need to adjust my mindset and techniques. I know I'm not the first person who let their ego get in the way of creating something or extending the process needed to achieve a sought-after goal.

Thinking back on my sophomore year at the University of Oregon, I can distinctly remember when one of our defensive captains and team leaders made a game-defining mistake! During the last minutes of a game against the Cal Bears, my teammate decided to blitz instead of executing his assignment to cover the running back when he went out for a pass. His mistake cost us the game. The next day when we gathered to watch film, he walked out of the meeting when that particular play came on screen! Yes, he walked out instead of sitting there and taking the feedback like the rest of us did. Even when you know you made a mistake, you must still keep your ego in check and allow yourself to hear the truth. We've all been there; we recognize the problem and now know how to fix it, so why listen to any assessment or feedback? You listen because it shows what type of character you have and that you are mature enough to take the feedback provided. It's also part of your job, showing your character during times of weakness. Are walking away or tuning out feedback the actions of a leader you would want to follow?

There are two different ways to get assessed: internally and externally. Internal assessments occur when *you* set up the parameters and give an honest assessment of where you are in your life.

The Wheel of Life (https://wheeloflife.io/) is an excellent assessment tool that you can customize and use to help gain more self-awareness, see where you're strong, and learn where you have the opportunity for growth in areas including health, money, family, spirituality, and five other regions. You can view where you are today and where you want to be in the future. In fact, a visual aid is a great tool to help many people see where they are at and where they want to go. I have created plenty of these in my time as a personal development coach. Job title, salary, free time, enjoying what you do, physical health, mental health, and spirituality are ways to assess how you quantify success. And YOU are the one who gets to answer these questions.

On the flipside, external assessments involve someone else evaluating your actions (your coach, significant other, boss, supervisor, etc.).

When executing assessment activities (internal or

external), it's beneficial to do so when you are not emotionally charged and can rather look through a non-biased lens with no feelings attached to the feedback.

When you absorb the information given to you (from a trusted and reliable source), you can accelerate your knowledge and growth.

WHO AND WHO NOT TO TAKE ADVICE FROM

During the first few months when I worked at Nike as a personal trainer, I was asked to teach a "Cardio Boxing" class. I was one of the only male trainers on campus, and I looked the part, so the head of the group fitness department deemed me "qualified." At first, I was very reluctant to leave my comfort zone. I was great one-on-one, but in a large group environment, felt very unsure of myself. After shadowing the class instructor a couple of times and learning how to set up and coach the class, I started to feel more confident in taking on the responsibility.

I taught the class for the first time and enjoyed overwhelming reviews (music was on point, the flow was excellent, and I was clear in my instructions). After I spent 3 weeks teaching the class 3 days per week, my supervisor Beth said she would watch and give me an assessment. I felt very confident when she walked in the door. I had been receiving great feedback from the class. What could go wrong…right?

Afterward, Beth and I sat down so she could give me

some "constructive feedback." She told me that the flow of the class was great, and I used the right cues to signal to the class what they were doing right and what they were doing wrong. This was music to my ears, as she had shared pretty much what I wanted to hear. But then she said, "Alex, you know you're teaching the class and not actually TAKING the class anymore. You should be walking around and coaching, not boxing and coaching at the same time." I was floored and embarrassed, and at first, closed myself off and felt defiant; but then I quickly took inventory on who was providing the feedback. It was someone who had bet on me, had my best interest at heart, and would look good if I looked good.

I thought the only feedback that mattered was from people taking the class, but that would be inherently biased based on how I made attendees feel with my positive words, upbeat music, prior interactions, and high energy level. Beth didn't care about how I made the class *feel*. Her sole focus was on if I helped people become more active in a safe environment while teaching them the foundations of boxing.

HIGH ACHIEVER NUGGETS:

- Ask yourself if the people assessing you have any biases.

- Can you trust that the person or people assessing you have your best interest at heart? What has their character revealed about them?

- Ask others if they have seen a change in you (if so, ask them to be specific) because your intentions to change for the better might not be outwardly apparent. Do your actions, behaviors, and words show you are evolving?

- Be aware of your ego obstructing your development. If you find yourself making comfortable choices, chances are your ego is getting in the way.

CHAPTER 7:

NO PLAN B

— ◇ —

When I was a trainer at Nike, I used to ask my clients all the time, "Are you the pig or the chicken?" They would look so puzzled when I first posed this question. Explaining the metaphor in greater detail, I'd go on to say, "If you wanted breakfast, which animal would be more committed to this goal? The chicken, who laid some eggs for your lovely omelet? Or the pig, who laid down his life so you can enjoy some bacon?" They would then understand my point of expressing the commitment required to reach their fitness goals.

One of the biggest things needed to reach your goals and aspirations is a commitment to the journey. This may come at a cost, though. Your safety net (your parents, degree, relationships you can "lean on" in case you don't achieve what you want) must be removed. The biggest thing that can rob people of becoming who they want to be is the mental "safety net" we often possess.

Al Everest was our special teams coach in 2000 when I was with the New Orleans Saints. It was Jim Haslett's first year as an NFL head coach, and he strived to construct a fantastic staff full of coaches who were hungry to lead and win. Early on that year, during one of our special teams meetings, Al noticed that not everyone on the Saints valued the importance of this specific unit. Al, a self-professed history buff, shared the story of the Vikings during the Middle Ages. He said that after docking and deboarding, the leaders would burn their ships to the ground to show the level of commitment required to succeed when aiming to take over a new province. I envisioned myself in the Vikings' shoes, seeing their only mode of transportation set ablaze with no option to head back home. Then, I started to think about how I played the game of football, every aspect of it. From that point forward, I began to play every snap like it was my last. I became more committed; but it wasn't just me. Our whole team set out to "burn the ships." We felt comfortable in the uncomfortable, training harder in the weight room, running extra after practice, and staying later to watch film. The result? We started winning! Because of Coach Everest's speech and the inspiration it provided, we did something no other Saints team had done before: We won a playoff game!

Lacking a plan B can make you more creative, and it can change who you are. You can start to become calloused to things that used to slow you down or hold you back: things like comfortable workouts, conversations about how "easy" something is, or how agreeable someone was when you offered your input on something. You can start to enjoy the sometimes-lonely process of personal development and turn self-doubt into self-confidence.

Hard work, creativity, and perseverance are valuable commodities that can spring from a "burn-the-ships" type of mindset. Case in point:

Brion Bethel:Brion played football for the Idaho State Bengals from 1992-1996. He earned his degree in Finance and Health Care Administration, and after two years of training, tryouts, and letdowns, decided to hang up his cleats and walk away from his dream of playing in the NFL. During the summertime, Brion would work! He dug ditches at a school, pumped gas at a gas station, stacked boxes at a warehouse, and then worked retail at a local Foot Locker (since he was on scholarship, he wasn't able to work during the school year due to NCAA rules). While at Foot Locker, Brion developed his customer service and sales skills. Before long, he was promoted to manager. He did all this while training for football and taking summer school classes! Brion knew what passion and commitment could do for someone who lacked experience or knowledge, and he also knew that hard work was the equalizer. Armed with this knowledge and putting his NFL dreams to rest, Brion applied for a finance manager job at a local car dealership. After the interview process, they asked him if he would consider a sales job instead. His personality, along with his sales experience, was a better fit for this position. The office manager asked Brion, "How much money do you need to make to start with?" Brion thought for a second, "I need to make $36,000." The office manager immediately replied, "What if you could make five times that?" Brion, flabbergasted, asked, "What do I need to do?" The manager said, "Just be yourself, come out and talk to people...do you."

When Brion wants something, he is locked in and focused. He doesn't give himself a way out. For him, it's a do-or-die mentality. His first month on the job, he made $8,000. The next month, this increased to $10,000. He thought to himself, "It can't be this easy; all I'm doing is being kind to people, shooting them straight, and outworking others." He applied the same success principle he used when playing football to his new line of work. Brion became such a great salesman that the owner asked him to take more of a leadership position within the company, saying, "We need you to make more people like you." This came with a significant pay cut, but he was able to enjoy health and dental benefits and a 401(k). He quickly rose up the totem pole, and when the owner made an ill-advised business decision that bankrupted the company, Brion was poised to purchase it and take over. He didn't have a backup plan, and because of that mindset, went on to enjoy a successful business career.

I believe you must be 100% committed to anything you want to be successful in. Suppose you have a backup plan or a "side hustle." Compartmentalize this in the back of your mind. Otherwise, you will become easily sidetracked.

A student-athlete's primary purpose is to receive an education. The "athlete" piece should be considered plan A1. I know the rigors of a student-athlete lifestyle firsthand (early workouts, training table, countless meeting hours, watching film, walkthroughs, playbooks, practices, etc.). I get it. If you are a student-athlete, that all comes with the commitment to fulfill your role, separating you from typical students and ordinary people! The sacrifices you make today will make you in high demand tomorrow. Industry executives love hiring student-athletes because they know they possess specific transferable skills that are hard to come by: skills like working as a team, taking responsibility for your role and the people affected by it, communicating, setting goals, overcoming adversity, resolving conflicts, and working hard.

WHEN TO START LOOKING FOR PLAN B
(IF ONE EXISTS)

When you have exhausted all of your efforts, knowledge, and expertise and have applied patience to something and are still not where you want to be (or have lost your passion for that goal), then it's time to think about your next opportunity. Understand this, though; individuals who pour everything they have into something typically have a hard time letting go. When the door is completely shut on a career as a professional athlete, business owner, or even a relationship, it's time to start digging into your subconscious mind to find that plan B. There are also times when you begin to visualize and explore other opportunities outside of your sport after enjoying a great level of success. Here are some examples:

Angel McCoughtry, a five-time WNBA All-Star, is one of women's basketball's most lethal scorers. But since women's basketball salaries have long paled in comparison to those of NBA stars, Angel and others have sought out additional methods to build a nest egg. Angel, 33, became a successful businesswoman by opening a chain of ice cream shops.

Mia Hamm, after enjoying one of the most storied careers in soccer history, entered the boardroom. She is part owner of the LAFC soccer team and also works with FC Barcelona and A.S. Roma. The Mia Hamm Foundation raises funds for bone marrow transplants and creates more opportunities for girls and women in sport.

Former running back Justin Forsett made one Pro Bowl during a nine-year NFL career and now tackles hygiene. Justin and some college teammates created ShowerPill, a disposable body wipe that replaces the need to shower multiple times a day. He appeared on the TV show *Shark Tank*, and although Justin did not leave with a deal, ShowerPill stirred enough interest to earn $15,000 in sales a few hours after the episode aired.

Marshawn Lynch returned to the NFL late in the 2019 season, but the running back known as "Beast Mode" was already making gains off the field. He launched Beast Mode

Apparel and became a restaurant owner at the foundation of a business "empire," according to *Ad Age*. Marshawn's most savvy business move might be his decision to save most of his NFL salary and live off money earned through endorsements.

As a two-time NBA champion with the Detroit Pistons, Vinnie Johnson was known as "The Microwave." But after his career, he became known for selling automotive parts. Piston Automotive supplies Ford and GM, growing from a single Detroit facility to a company with locations across the Midwest.

HIGH ACHIEVER COACHING QUESTIONS:

- What level of commitment do you need to reach your goal(s)?

- What can you do to compartmentalize your plan A and bury plan B in the back of your mind?

- How can you mentally remove a safety net that might be in place if you fail (family members, relationships, backup job, etc.)?

- What transferable skills do you have because of the sport you play(ed) (e.g., communication, relationship building, teamwork, decision making, etc.)?

CHAPTER 8:

THE POWER OF ENVIRONMENTS

— ◇ —

Your environment is more powerful than you might think. It shapes and molds you, and if you're not careful, it can slowly turn you into the person you most despise. It can also transform you into the person you most admire. Still, you must recognize your environment and how it affects you emotionally, economically, and spiritually. Is it shaping you into the person you want to become? This starts with having a vision for your future self.Many movies and stories depict people overcoming their environments and living the lives they always dreamed of. Yet, many real-life stories are not all that popular, but in fact heartbreaking.

Case Study: Athlete #1

This athlete was a superstar football player who had college offers coming out the ying-yang! He wasn't a fan of the recruiting process. Football was his release. But to truly realize why it was his release, you need to understand what he was trying to escape: his home life. His family's construction business failed in the early 2000s, and they endured legal and financial troubles. His parents divorced while he was in elementary school, and he began to split time between two households.

At one point, his father vanished for months before reappearing in his native state. This young and impressionable boy was forced to become the man of the house in his early teens. His mother was on disability, unable to watch over him at times. He often had to take care of himself.

By the spring of his junior year in high school, he had burned out. Frustrated by the challenges of recruiting, school, and home life, including his father's absence, he (in a fit of teen irrationality) considered giving up his dream of being a college athlete.

Although described as a good kid with good intentions, he was no angel. Girls were after him, and he was perfectly okay with that. Sometimes he partied too much. At times, his priorities were out of whack. It was a struggle for him to stay focused while having free rein at home. His grades suffered because he missed weeks of school at a time. He started hanging around guys with bad intentions. They influenced him to start smoking weed and drinking alcohol.

When he finally decided to attend a top-ten college football program, he was more mature...or so he thought.

"The common theme is if you create the structure and support for him, he'll have success," one coach had said. "He's proven, when he's traveled that path within that structure and maintained within those boundaries, he can do well."

His high school counselor had some doubts, wondering if he still lacked faith in his abilities to succeed.

"I wish I felt more confident," she said. "He has work to do. I'm hopeful, and I know he can do it. It's just a matter of him keeping his focus and being mindful of his environment. Unfortunately, we have to be on him all of the time."

This athlete found some success as a true freshman. His sophomore campaign was even better, but before his junior year, his head coach left for the NFL. The structure and discipline he provided left with him.

Athlete #1 broke team rules and was suspended for the first two games of the season. He wound up quitting the team. He got a shot as a rookie free agent, but his dream of having a long NFL career was short-lived due to a knee injury he suffered in practice. He continued to chase his goal with stints in the arena football league and Canadian Football League.

Now out of the "league" and with no structure or guidance, he began using drugs. The police caught him with cocaine. Later on, he was found with heroin and then got a DUI. The final straw was a domestic abuse arrest. He is now serving a two-year prison sentence.

Case Study: Athlete #2

This athlete is a female basketball player for a Division II college. She was an okay athlete and had a vision of herself as more than this. She was a late bloomer in terms of her basketball skills but made up for it with her leadership, drive, and work ethic. When she finished college, she wanted to work in sports marketing.She shared great friendships with all of her teammates, but she also wanted to get to know more people outside of her team. She thought about joining a sorority but assumed it would put too much on her plate as a student-athlete.

She started hanging with some friends outside of her sport, from the area where she grew up. They had a lot of similarities, other than what they perceived as fun.

These friends liked frequenting house parties and their small nightclub in town, which she thought was okay. When they started drinking alcohol and smoking marijuana in front of her, she felt a strong sense of negative peer pressure. I say negative because positive peer pressure can influence us as well.

Positive peer pressure exists when your friends say something like, "Hey, let's go to the library and hit these books before we head to the movies. We have to ace this test so we don't have to go to study hall anymore."

After telling her friends that smoking and drinking was not something she's cool with, she quickly realized that not everyone will be on the same wavelength as her. She soon started to distance herself from them. She had a vision that was more substantial than her desire to have friends outside of her sport.

Humans have a strong need for safety and security, and we look for these attributes in our environment. We look for physical comforts, such as an environment with the right temperature. But more importantly, we seek a psychologically comfortable environment: for example, domains that are familiar but offer the right amount of stimulus.

Athlete #2 didn't like the stimulus that was offered, so she chose to walk away. Many of us stay in the wrong environment because we lack a strong enough sense of self and are more concerned with pleasing others than ourselves.

DESIGN YOUR SURROUNDINGS TO MAKE GOOD CHOICES

We often think that achieving a task involves just getting out there and doing it. We believe that if there's a will, we can find a way towards a goal. Yet, it's our environment, not just us, that dictates what we choose to do.

If choices surround you that are distracting or lead to bad decisions, it becomes hard to make the right ones. On the flip side, an environment containing only desirable options might constrict you from doing what's vital for yourself. If you want to improve your habits, take a deep and prolonged look around and see how you can make things easier or more convenient for yourself.

For instance:

- To get homework done, minimize distractions that steal focus from the task at hand.

- When persuading someone to help you, explain and set up what you need, decreasing the chance for error.

- If you want to eat better, keep healthier foods and water close at hand.

- If you want to add more diversity to your environment, choose non-athletes to hang around. You will be surprised at how many people will accept you.

The desire to get something done is just the tip of the iceberg. If you seek a particular outcome, you need an environment that brings you closer to accomplishing your goal.

CHANGING YOURSELF BEGINS WITH CHANGING YOUR ENVIRONMENT

Making changes to your environment makes it easier to do what's right without the need to consciously think about staying motivated. If you construct your environment so that making the best decisions comes easily, you can set yourself up to practice better habits.

Often, we think that change comes from within. We believe that achieving a goal is about changing ourselves and what we believe. Yet, we discount the fact that optimizing our environment to make better choices can significantly impact our actions. Having a better option within reach makes it the default choice.

RECOGNIZING THE INTERNAL ENVIRONMENT YOU WANT TO CREATE

A 2015 study by Robin M. Scholefield, Ph.D., and Dylan M. Firsick, Ph.D. (University of Southern California) found that mindfulness helps teach awareness and understanding of emotions in the present moment with a non-judgmental approach to one's experiences. They created a five-session program to teach relaxation, present-focused awareness, and acceptance of thoughts and emotions.

Their goals were to reduce anxiety, increase well-being, and improve mindfulness ability among student-athletes. The five main topics covered were:

- Introduction to Mindfulness

- Mindfulness of the Body

- Emotions

- Thoughts

- Building a Mindfulness Practice

Key Findings:

- 12 women and 24 men (N=36) from five Division I teams completed the program-Found significant declines in anxiety, increases in overall well-being, and improved mindfulness ability by the 5th session-Pre-Program Mindfulness: 64% of participants did not practice mindfulness-Post-Program Mindfulness:

- 89% practiced related to sport; 40% practiced 5-10+ times

- 71% practiced outside sport; 23% practiced 5-10+ times

After initial training, mindfulness (perhaps better known as "meditating") can continue in as little as five minutes a day, quickly integrating into one's lifestyle without adding to an already overloaded student-athlete schedule. The strength of this program is its adaptability and ease of implementation. Participants found that mindfulness, as a practice, does not require specialized equipment, customized facilities, or uniform procedures. You can just roll out of bed and do it!Later on in his career, Kobe Bryant would dedicate 10 minutes of his day to meditation, saying, "It anchors me throughout my day."

It's pretty simple to find out which internal environment is the best fit for you. The hardest part is being intentional in finding it. Think about the times when you did great on a test, said the right words to someone you were attracted to, or enjoyed your best performance in your sport.

One of the best seasons I ever had was when I added meditation to my daily schedule. In that season (my 7th in the NFL), there was a young first-round draft pick nipping at my heels to get on the field. I played out of position for part of the year, was still healing from my previous years' surgeries, and was playing on a veteran's minimum salary of $550,000 (if I played 95% of defensive snaps, I would get a $1,400,000 bonus!). The pressure was on, but because of the choice I made to change my internal environment, I wound up having the best year of my career despite the external environment around me (that I had no control over).

EXTERNAL ENVIRONMENT

While at the University of Oregon, we held a different type of practice on Thursdays wherein we would pipe artificial crowd noise into the stadium. It was deafening for an hour and 45 minutes. At first, we all had a tough time dealing with the distraction of not being able to hear our teammates or coaches, but it forced us to use our alternate form of communication: hand signals. The way we practiced and communicated was the main reason that season was our best in 37 years!

You can become accustomed to any environment, good or bad. It all depends on choice. After my freshman year at Oregon, I went back home to Colorado Springs to stay with my mom and stepdad.

They had a very dysfunctional marriage as alcoholics with a history of domestic abuse. However, I was extremely homesick and wanted to re-energize for the summer, so I went home.

During my time back at home, my stepdad got into an altercation with my twin brother. My brother was smaller in stature, and my stepdad (a former Army veteran) was bigger and tougher than him. I heard some banging downstairs, like someone was thrown against a wall. I lost it; I saw RED! I flew down the stairs and started beating the shit out of my stepdad. I'm not proud of that moment in my life, but it taught me something vital about myself. I don't like cliches like saying someone was "acting out of character." The character is always there! It's the *environment* that can bring out the monster in people. In that environment, when a man threatened my mom and my brother, that monster came out in me, and "it" could have potentially killed someone.

I recognized this, and before returning to school, found myself with a restraining order against me, courtesy of my stepdad. For two weeks, I slept on the couch at a friend's house. I didn't go back home after that incident until my mother divorced him three years later.

I decided not to return to that environment because I knew what type of monster I could become if put in that situation again. I had a choice, just like so many others. My intention was centered on what I wanted to do and where I wanted to go—graduate and possibly play in the NFL—not the relationship I had with my mother. So many of us feel stuck because our family members are stuck, but they don't know how or have the desire to change their environment. I couldn't force my mom to leave that man. She had to figure that out on her own.

HIGH ACHIEVER COACHING QUESTIONS:

- Which type of internal environment do you want to create for yourself?

- Is it even important to you?

- How can you design your environment to make it as convenient as possible to have success?

- Take inventory of your external environment. Does it align with what you want to achieve?

- Are there people in your life you should separate or distance yourself from (family included)?

- Do you know which external environment has given you the most success? Conversely, do you recognize the environment that can bring out your absolute worst character?

CHAPTER 9:

DEVELOPING YOUR OWN PROCEDURES

— ◇ —

I don't know about you, but the word "procedure" has a negative connotation for me. Maybe it's because I've undergone so many medical procedures or because of the technical feeling it invokes. Have you ever worked at a fast-food restaurant, in landscaping, or maybe in a department store? Typically, the manager teaches employees procedures and protocols, or the fundamentals, of their role. This probably isn't sexy or glamorous, but it is essential to operate a profitable business and just part of the job. If employed in this way, you probably needed to follow procedures that provided essential information, and in turn, solid foundation, to find success. Trying to carry out your assignment based on how you "feel" can be dangerous.

In 1992, I played in the Independence Bowl. It was the second bowl game in 20 years the Oregon Ducks had appeared in. I was amped up, as you can imagine. It was my first time playing on national television. My entire family was watching the game. We were dominating the Wake Forest Demon Deacons 22-10. At the beginning of the third quarter,

I "jumped" a flat route, intercepted the ball, and basically walked into the end zone! I celebrated with my teammates, yelled "Hi mom!" into the camera following me, and soaked in all of the glory.

Twenty minutes later, something catastrophic happened.

I was back on the field. I didn't follow my procedure. I didn't focus my eyes on the receiver after reading it was a run. The receiver plowed into my knee. I didn't even see him. The next thing I knew, I was on my back, writhing in pain. I remember the ref blowing the whistle, my teammates all around me, and the trainers running out and testing my left leg for stability. I tried to get up and walk, but my body said otherwise. I collapsed to the ground. It turns out that I had torn my anterior cruciate ligament, lateral cruciate ligament, and severely stretched my posterior cruciate ligament. I was devastated, and, in my mind, coming face-to-face with the end of my athletic career. A couple weeks later, I had reconstructive surgery on my left knee. It required two screws and a graft of my patellar tendon, leaving two scars behind (8 inches and 2 inches long). I was rehabbing back home in Eugene when I finally built up enough courage to watch the film. What I saw wasn't exactly how I remembered it. I recalled being the recipient of a cheap shot, courtesy of the Wake Forest wide receiver. I felt angry and pissed off at this asshole of a football player, but after watching the play from a birds-eye view, realized it was in fact me who had not followed the proper procedure.

We had been taught to read run or pass, and your

responsibility would change based on that information. If a pass, you would backpedal or turn and run to protect against the deep ball. If a run, you would:

1. Put your eyes on the receiver

2. Defeat the block (stock or chop)

3. Make the tackle or force the ball inside

With the fresh Pick 6 in my mind, I thought I could just skip the procedure I had been coached on. The early success I enjoyed in the game had gone to my head. I wanted to make another big play. I wanted to hear my name called on the stadium intercom. I wanted the television announcers to say my name, talk about me, shower me with compliments, and even mention my high school alma mater.

That way of thinking cost me dearly.

Has something like this ever happened to you? Have you ever skipped a procedure at school, work, or on your team? Have you taken your eyes off of your primary goal, role, or objective? Did you skip a step because of your success or even failure?Here are some questions you can ask yourself when it comes to following procedures:

- Is the system proven?

- Is the person or group who developed the procedure credible?

- Is there another system, protocol, or procedure you can use?

- If you don't follow the system, what are potential consequences?

FUNDAMENTALS ARE ESSENTIAL, NOT BASIC

Learning the fundamentals of your sport, weightlifting, or working on a class project is not about grasping the basics; it's about learning and processing the essential elements of those things. Fundamentals are not basic factors you can just toss aside; rather, they are essential to find success. If you lack the fundamentals, you lack a solid foundation and are susceptible to injury, setbacks, and wasted time and energy.

While in college, I witnessed many of my teammates omitting procedures necessary to achieve a passing grade in class. For example, they would skip or leave class early. This would lead to a failing grade, placing them on academic probation. When this happened, you had to attend study hall. Study hall was mandatory for two types of student-athletes:

1. Freshman

2. Anyone on academic probation (<2.5 GPA)

The discipline they displayed on the field did not show up in the classroom. I can remember watching my teammates roll hundreds of yards on the football field, throw up from the dizziness, then roll some more and skip class. Coaches would secretly attend class for them, get caught, and face discipline.The procedure to gain the most success out of your college experience requires you to go to class (for the whole duration), take notes, participate, and learn. If you skip related procedures, you can quickly end up wasting a beautiful opportunity that can be life-altering. Student-athletes have structure when with their team, at practice, or in the weight room. But when in class or study hall, that same discipline and structure must be maintained.One of the saddest things I encountered was when some of my teammates attended college for four to five years, only to walk away with no degree and nothing to show for their time and effort beyond their memories. Some would find jobs but could never take on a managerial or executive position because they didn't meet the educational requirements to do so. They didn't earn their degrees. All because they lacked discipline and didn't follow procedures.

FRESHMAN FREEDOM

I arrived at Eugene early. Back in the 1990s, this meant joining team workouts in July as a freshman. I was able to get a job at a steel mill, work out with my team, and live in a house with a couple of upperclassmen teammates. I had so much freedom, I almost felt like a professional athlete. I would work, work out, and at the end of the day, hang out with the fellas. I did this for a month before the rest of the team reported to training camp.

There was more structure when camp started. Oregon

was on the quarter system, which meant school didn't start until the last week in September. This meant that until that time, I would think, eat, and drink only football. We had three games before school started, and since I was redshirting, felt like I was living my best life. I was partying, eating everything in sight, and skipping classes. I figured since I was only practicing and not playing in games, I would enjoy all of this newfound freedom.

By the end of the quarter, I had gained 17 pounds (primarily fat), and my GPA was a dismal 1.87!

I was scared to death! I had promised my mom that I would get a degree. I had a full-ride scholarship to a major university and was about to blow the opportunity of a lifetime! I was placed on academic probation, which meant I had to meet with my academic advisor once per week. My coach was informed, so he would also most likely check in on me from time to time to make sure I went to class.My newfound freedom was restricted, I had more structure, and now the wrath of my mom in the back of my mind. Needless to say, this forced me to focus. I followed the procedures and protocols outlined by my academic advisors, coaches, and mom. The thought of returning home as someone who "blew it in college," plus all of the things I just mentioned motivated me to get my academics back on track. I ended up earning a 3.3 the next semester, shedding the need for academic probation. That would be the one and only time I was on that list.

HIGH ACHIEVER COACHING POINTS:

- Who would you impact (other than yourself) if you didn't follow procedures in and out of your sport?

- What would motivate you to have success in the classroom?

- Which freedoms would you sacrifice to revel in short-term pleasure?

- What type of discipline is needed for you to graduate? Does this vary from discipline employed in your sport?

Regardless of success or failure, stick with a proven procedure. Be patient, believe in the system, and let success come to you. Don't chase it!

CHAPTER 10:

CREATING RELATIONSHIP ROADMAPS

— ◇ —

Roadmaps are helpful when it comes to locating and commuting to specific destinations.

Before all of this magnificent technology we now have in our vehicles, we used literal roadmaps to get us where we wanted to go. I remember driving from Detroit, Michigan, to Colorado Springs, Colorado in a Datsun! My dad was driving, and my mom was the "navigator." She had this crinkly old roadmap she had grabbed at a gas station, but it helped us find our destination in the shortest time possible.

In this chapter, I'm going to provide a roadmap for building relationships. But just like my pops, you have to first figure out where you want to go before starting your journey, understanding what type of character it will take to get there.

When you have integrity and good character, opportunities sometimes appear or fall into your lap. When my family and I moved to Portland, Oregon, the only people I knew were my in-laws and a couple of my old University of Oregon teammates. One of my close teammates told me I should connect with the Oregon Alumni Association, a great networking resource. I became a member, and shortly thereafter, was contacted to play in a "Legends" golf tournament. I thought it would be cool to see some of my former teammates and other Oregon athletes and network with alumni, so I accepted.

I later learned that each golf team had a chance to bid on their "legend," which I thought was pretty neat. I was also humbled, as the group had paid $5,000 to have me join their team!

During our 5 hours playing golf together, we got a chance to know each other. The others had tons of questions about my playing days, both in college and the league. I had questions for them as well. I asked each how they got started in their industry. Everyone shared varied and exciting stories. Some fell into a family business. Others found a passion and pursued it. We also talked about family, and my five kids were the hot topic for a good 30 minutes.I had a blast playing golf, sharing stories with the fellas, and making new friends. We exchanged numbers and agreed to stay in touch with one another.

Fast forward six months, and I had a job interview for a personal training position at Nike World Headquarters, which boasted two world-class fitness centers. The interview went great, I thought, as the woman I met with asked me back the next day to train her and another trainer. I went back to the facility and led them in a well-thought-out workout. Afterwards, she said, "Alex, that was a great workout, but you know you had this job wrapped up a long time ago, right?"

I was confused. "You played golf with my husband at the University of Oregon Legends tournament. He went on and on about what a great person you are, what high integrity you showed, and how refreshing it was to be with someone who wasn't caught up in his own celebrity."

Because of the person I was and the character I had displayed, I was able to get a job at the largest sportswear company in the world, become a consultant for the organization, collaborate on a Nike/Xbox video game, and travel the world while training and sharing the stage with superstar athletes. If I didn't show up with integrity, be myself, interact with new people, and share stories, there is no way I would have been able to secure that position.

How you communicate with people matters tremendously. Your first interaction with someone, no matter if they're trying to sell you something or even if they're serving you, is the best they will ever treat you. For example, if you walk into a car dealership and the service is not excellent from the beginning, then most likely, you can expect a terrible experience if you need to return for car service in the future.

So, my advice to you is:

1. Treat everybody with respect. Just because you are viewed as a celebrity, doesn't give you the right to act like a jerk.

2. Be intentional in how you want others to feel when they interact with you.

3. Listen with intention and speak to understand, not to one-up someone.

4. Be mindful of your first interaction with people because it will be the best they ever treat you.

Astor Chambers was a high school senior in 1992. He was also a stud basketball player and class president at the world-renowned Fiorello H. LaGuardia High School in New York City (the 1980s television show *Fame* was based on this performing arts school). One day, Astor was asked to give a tour to a visitor interested in the connection between sport and art in New York City. He did so without knowing who exactly the person was. Her name was Betsy. She asked him questions about fashion and the shoes he was wearing (Nike Air Max). She wondered why he had bought these particular shoes, assuming it was due to the cushioning, fit, or technology, but none of those things mattered to him and his peers. What mattered was they looked dope! Alongside the colors, the fact that Nike had transformed a running shoe it into a fashion statement was the kicker. This was all pertinent news to this young white lady from Portland, Oregon, (who was living in New York) to hold focus groups and then take research findings back to the Nike World campus.She and Astor became good friends, and she would often come back to the area, gift him new kicks, and ask for his feedback on what made the product so dope. He would later ask her how he could get his foot in the door at Nike. She told him to find a retail job. He took her advice and worked at a local Foot Locker in college. While there, he learned the fundamentals of sales, marketing, and merchandise, which helped him land his first role within Nike, an EKIN role. EKIN program members served as the liaison between varied storefronts (e.g., Nike town, Footlocker, Dr. J's, Modell's sporting goods, Jimmy Jazz, or Footaction).They are responsible for informing consumers about brand technology and story behind Nike products. Astor had assumed that playing in the NBA or overseas was a long shot due to his stature (he was 5'9"). Instead, he focused on making better and deeper connections at Nike.

Astor kept in touch with Betsy Parker (the sister of Mark Parker, former President of Nike), who would continue to serve as a voice for Astor when he wasn't present.

That career went on to take Astor worldwide, working for other companies such Adidas, most recently Beats by Dre', Billionaire Boy's Club and collaborating with Kanye West, Yara Shahidi, Beyonce Knowles, Pusha-T, and Pharrell Williams.

And to think, all of this wouldn't have happened if he hadn't been himself (someone of integrity, friendly, and approachable) while taking that "lady" on a tour of his school. You never know who you can impact and who can impact you in return!In another case, "Athlete C" was an accomplished high school athlete from Southern California. He had prototypical size, speed, and athleticism for a wide receiver heading into a college football program. He made some amazing plays in a limited role his freshman year. As a sophomore, he became a full-time starter and made a name for himself both on and off the field. Athlete C was into the ladies and quickly became known as a womanizer. He came to recognize his on-campus fame and began relying too heavily on his God-given athletic ability. He began to skip his workouts, take plays off, and choose younger, inexperienced guys to work against in competitive practice periods.

He also started treating people differently. If you had status on the team, were a big-time booster, or a coach who could help improve his stock in the NFL, he would befriend you. He would quickly turn these ties into transactional relationships. As a large part of these transactions, if you "earned" the right to be in his presence, you would be asked to do something for him in return.

As you can probably figure out, many people developed a disdain for Athlete C and his actions. The word spread to many alumni, who began to distance themselves from him. When NFL executives, scouts, and coaches asked questions about his character and work ethic, coaches who once had high hopes for him both on and off the field told the truth. He got a shot as a rookie free agent (prior to his senior season, he had been projected as a second or third-round draft pick) but was often injured in training camp and released soon after.

Athlete C returned to his college town and reached out to boosters and alumni, seeking an entry-level job within their companies. These same people who used to cheer for him now avoided him. They learned the type of individual he was without the spotlight and the uniform.

This story is an excellent illustration of what not to do when trying to make meaningful relationships as a college student-athlete. When blessed with this platform (what you do), why not use this to your advantage? You can use it as a vehicle to bond with people in high positions who are very connected; but you must be genuine and upfront in your intentions.

Garren Strong played football for the University of Oregon from 2004-2008. Following a win, he went into the locker room and spotted Nike co-founder Phil Knight! Something told Garren to go over and introduce himself.

"Something came over me, and I went to go introduce myself to 'Uncle Phil.' Of course, he knew all of us by name, but we never formally introduced ourselves to him. We would say hi and keep it rollin'. He was iconic." How many times have you been in the proximity of someone with a ton of professional success but never dared to say hello, strike up a conversation, or ask how they were doing?

Garren continued, "I went up to him and said, 'Hi, my name is Garren Strong.'"

Uncle Phil cut him off and said, "I know who you are."

"Yes, but I wanted to officially introduce myself to you and tell you that I would love the opportunity to work for your company someday."

Phil paused for a moment before saying, "Get in touch with Jim Bartko (assistant athletic director at the time) to set up a meeting to learn what you'd want to do and have an interest in."

A couple days later, Garren stopped by Jim's office.

"Hey, Jim!" He was immediately interrupted by Mr. Bartko. "Phil Knight told me you were going to stop by."Phil Knight was by no means obligated to tell Jim Bartko that Garren Strong would stop by his office to have a conversation, but because of the impact Garren made on Phil in his simple formal introduction, he was able to plant a seed.

Upon graduating, Garren was offered a 12-month internship at Nike (every year, 20,000 college students apply, but only 250 get accepted). His discipline, time management, leadership, accountability, and team dynamics played a role in his decision to take that internship and parlay it into a career in brand marketing for Nike and Jordan.

In doing so, Garren was able to think past his hopes and dreams of playing in the NFL.

"I had to be real with myself. I knew only the top 1% of guys can play at that level."

Garren was a realist. He thought about starting his career

early on and paid close attention to athletes in other sports who would come back into town to work out.

"They would bounce around in their sport, whether it was the NBA G-league, baseball minor leagues, or NFL practice squads, and had nothing to show for it. They had no real money: just cool stories!"

HIGH ACHIEVER COACHING QUESTIONS:

- How do you approach connecting with others? First, you need to connect with yourself. Learn your passions, skills, and opportunities for growth. In the previous chapter (Assignment), we discussed finding your purpose and how to go about doing so; ask yourself what you enjoy doing, what you excel at, what the world needs more of, and if you can get paid to do that.

- How can you get to know people for the sake of doing so? You may learn something about an individual you might not like and choose not to associate with them to avoid adverse effects on you and your brand.

- How can you add value when meeting new people? This may take shape as a simple conversation or even an ask to serve (such as a free internship).

You can meet people at networking events, conferences, mastermind groups, etc. Perhaps the best way is to *have someone you know to introduce you* (warm introductions are the *most* impactful).

CHAPTER 11:

USING ADVERSITY AS AN ADVANTAGE

— ◇ —

Adversity is inevitable. You know it, I know it, a baby first learning how to walk knows it. But what if I told you that the adversity you're facing right now or have already experienced could be your most significant advantage? On the flip side, what if your biggest advantage could be your greatest disadvantage? Let me explain.

THE INJURY BUG

The risk of injury for a student-athlete is something that cannot be denied. Statistics reveal that 90 percent of student-athletes report some kind of sports-related injury, while 54 percent report they have played while hurt.

In a previous story, I shared how I tore up my knee during our 1992 bowl game. That single incident was the primary reason I was able to get drafted so high and play as long as I did in the NFL. Now, I certainly wouldn't want to go through that again, nor would I wish my injury on anyone else. But that perceived disadvantage was my most significant advantage.

When I started walking again (without crutches), I worked with Coach James Radcliffe. "Coach Rad" was a thirty-year-old human bouncy ball. He was 5'8", 165 lbs of pure spring. Little did I know that he was a pioneer in plyometric training. He taught seminars in dozens of countries, wrote books, and produced plyometric training videos that are sold worldwide.

For one of our first rehab sessions, I remember showing up at 6:30 am. The sun was rising in the corner of the end zone. I could still see my breath walking to the stadium. I remember being determined to attack my rehab and progress in leaps and bounds rather than tiny increments. I entered the stadium, and Coach Radcliffe and I were the only ones out there. Lights flickered as I stood before him, waiting for his first order. "Walk," he said. He had me walk with extreme precision. I walked ten yards, forward and backward, for an hour. First, he had me focus on my lower-body mechanics; then, my upper body, before syncing everything together. My hips were on fire, as well as my ears. "Knee up...toe up...heel up, Alex. Arms at 90 degrees, relaxed hands, hands cheek to cheek!" I felt like Daniel Son coached by Mr. Miyagi in the first *Karate Kid* movie. "Wax on, wax off."

Everything he taught me was built on understanding and applying the same principles as part of a mounting "building block" of skill. Walk, march, skip, and then run, in that order. This way of training was all foreign to me. The only formal sprinting skill work I had ever done was with my high school track coach. Coach Rad broke everything down so I could understand it. He would often say, "Alex, when you understand things at the foundational level, you can then own it."

When was the last time you understood something at the foundational level? It is easy to skip steps when we're trying to grow and improve at something, and in many situations, skipping steps is not only glorified but expected.

Because of the 1:1 coaching I received from Coach Radcliffe (6 months, 4 days per week, 1 hour per day), I improved my time from 4.46 to 4.32 in a forty-yard sprint and increased my vertical jump by 3.5 inches (38 inches to 41.5). It took me 16 months to fully recover, but I came back and started an entire season after only eight months of rehab: eight months spent building a stronger foundation.

It didn't stop there. Because of the overall speed I had lost when returning after only eight months of rehab, I had to watch more film, ask more questions, and listen more intently at practice and games. In the long run, I gained so much more than just speed and athleticism because of my injury; I also increased my football IQ. Your sports IQ can help you in the short and long-term of your athletic career. Getting smarter is always a good thing!

THE COACHING CAROUSEL

The idea of having one position coach or one head coach sounds magnificent, and it's something coaches use to recruit prospective student-athletes. It provides parents and student-athletes with a sense of stability and normalcy. Yet, more often than not, an athlete may be exposed to a new head coach or position coach while they're in college. No matter the sport, the likelihood of having the same coach is rare. Since 2016, there have been 89 new head coaching hires at NCAA Division I football schools. Some coaches retire, find media jobs as commentators or analysts, or ascend to the NFL ranks, but most are unfortunately fired.

During my five years at Oregon, I had three head coaches, three defensive backs coaches, and three defensive coordinators. All of them had different philosophies, techniques, and verbiage. If you didn't pay attention to one coaching point, you would be lost, frustrating coaches and teammates in their quest to win.I learned different coaching styles, communication, and overall knowledge from my various coaches. My first defensive backs coach was Denny Schuler. I thought he didn't like me at first. In fact, I thought he hated me! But I later learned he was tougher on younger players who had the potential to play early on. I also learned how to ask questions respectively and stick up for myself. My second defensive backs coach, Coach Nick Aliotti, was cut from a different cloth. During a time when some of my teammates thought he was showing favoritism, he said, "You damn right I have favorites...the players that give 100% are coachable, make plays, and have no excuses...you damn right...those are my favorite players!" He taught us to learn and have fun in every situation on the football field, in the locker room, and in the meeting rooms.

Coach Charlie Waters was my last defensive coordinator and defensive backs coach in college. He had spent over 20 years playing and coaching in the NFL (Dallas Cowboys and Denver Broncos, respectively). Charlie taught me to believe in my skills and how to be a leader on the field. He once told me, "Alex, you need to be my coach on the field, and you need to bring the younger guys up to your level." The first question I asked him was, "How do I do that?" He replied, "You have to connect with them, spend time with them, help them see the bigger picture of what we are trying to do as a defensive unit, but most of all, you need to show them how to be accountable." I replied, "What do you mean by that?" He said, "Have no excuses, absolutely NONE!""None?" He replied, "Not-a-one."

What if I didn't get the defensive play call? What if the defense called was wrong? What if I played injured during a game, and because of that injury, sucked and hurt the team? What if my dog ate my playbook?Your fault, your fault, your fault, and your fault.

"You didn't get the play call? Call a timeout or tell us you didn't get it."

"If the defense called was wrong, make it right and get everyone to play the same defense. It's up to you to make sure you know the strength and weakness of every play call."

109

"You played injured and you sucked? Your fault. Nobody put a gun to your head. Let us know you can't go."

"Dog ate your playbook? Do a better job training your dog or know which dog breeds eat playbooks."

Charlie was a great coach. Instead of feeling sorry for myself given the perceived lack of stability associated with the coaching changes, I decided to consider this an opportunity to learn new ways of thinking, communicating, and building relationships.

If you are a student-athlete who is heading to college or already there, you will most likely have a new coach or two by the time you leave. What type of attitude will you adopt to succeed in your sport if this happens? Will you be open to learning new concepts and systems to help your team? Will you look to transfer or stay put if coaching changes arise? What excuses can you eliminate to be fully accountable? In the "real world," change is constant. If you decide to work in a corporate, non-profit, or even entrepreneur sector, you must not only adapt but develop a positive attitude towards change. Will you have the tools necessary to help you navigate this accordingly?

RELATIONSHIPS

My first college roommate played on the University of Oregon basketball team. We were both from Colorado and became friends the summer before we reported to college. He was a

McDonald's All-American point guard who took his high school team to the Colorado State Championship four years straight, winning three titles. A 6-foot-3, strong, thick-bodied guard, he was a magician with the basketball. He was a point guard who could—as one player who guarded him in a state title game had said—"make the ball disappear." He averaged over 30 points for two straight years and had eight 50-point games. Many called him the greatest basketball player to ever come out of Colorado. He had a ton of hype going into college and was expected to not only start for the Ducks but play a significant role on the team.He had a girlfriend back home in Colorado, and they would talk on the phone until midnight or later, listening to Jodeci while chatting. Sometimes, they would fight. Other times, they would be lovey-dovey with each other. He would tell me all the bad stuff that was going on in their relationship, and their lack of trust in one another was laughable. This occurred during the preseason when the basketball team wasn't playing games or even in school yet.

Once their basketball season got into full swing, I could tell he was not himself. The long phone calls, classes, and subsequent workload increased. He was smack dab in the middle of life as a student-athlete, which was taking a heavy toll on him. He wasn't playing well, his relationship with his girlfriend was on the rocks, and I couldn't stand him as a roommate (we in fact got into a physical altercation at one point). I moved out soon after. He ended up getting benched for most of the season and averaged six points per game during his two-year career at Oregon. I didn't see him much on campus and later found out he had dropped out of school to go back home.

The adversity he faced in his relationships with both his girlfriend and me was terrible. Yet, the primary relationship that caused the most friction was the one he had with himself. All he knew was basketball, and when that started to falter, he didn't know how to react. He lashed out at his girlfriend, and when that wasn't enough, he would often lash out at me.He only saw himself as a hooper, not even a student-athlete — just an athlete. In life, your most significant relationship is the one you share with yourself. Therefore, it's important to get to know yourself at a deeper level. Here are some questions for student-athletes, specifically:-What motivates you?-What other things besides sports make you happy?-Is there anything else that you're good at?-How do you want to be treated?-Do you reciprocate when you're interacting with others?-Do you have the character needed to engage in a long-distance relationship while in college?

These are just a few questions you need to ask yourself when trying to figure out who you are.

HIGH ACHIEVER NUGGETS:

- The same things that can give you an advantage can also be disadvantages.

- Growing up with privileges like enjoying a great

home life, access to resources like athletic training and coaching, great teachers, and wonderful schools can lead you to take these things for granted.

- Athletes are notorious for having the ability to block out distractions when in stressful environments. But on the other side of that coin, these same athletes can have tunnel vision and focus too much on results, which is sometimes a negative.

- Growing up in an environment without resources — like knowing the lights might be turned off because your mom couldn't pay the electric bill, scarce food options, a lack of parental love/guidance, or even the possibility of abuse in the home — can harden you and make you more resilient. Those disadvantages can be a huge advantage, but it all depends on the character of the person enduring these situations.

Your character can either spiral you into the depths of anger, self-hate, abuse, and suffering, or push you toward people and places you've only dreamed of. It can also shape how you view the world; but it is a choice! How do *you* want to employ any adversity nuggets in your life?

Steps to locate and leverage adversity nuggets:

- What kinds of adversity have you encountered in your life?

- Did that adversity help or hinder your growth?

- If it hindered your growth, how? Try not to place blame.

- If it helped in your growth, how? Be specific.

The same thing can be said about teams. Facing disadvantages as a team is the best way to become stronger. This is why good coaches try to create unfavorable conditions wherever and whenever they can. Your environment can shape you, but *you* get to decide if it will affect you positively or negatively.

CHAPTER 12:

EVOLVING YOUR STANDARDS

— ◇ —

When someone mentions "the rules of this class" or "the rules that we follow," this gives off a negative vibe. Plus, rules are in fact sometimes made to be broken. My mom, dad, and most definitely my grammy had rules. Rules like: no running in the house, ask to be excused from the dinner table, make your bed, or come home before the street lights come on. Any time I heard the word "rule" as a child, it made me feel restricted. Although I understood it was for a good reason, it still meant something negative in my mind.

A standard is different than a rule. A standard dictates what you do, and you act accordingly. Consider a bar for a high jumper. It can be raised or lowered depending on ability, and as high jumpers get stronger, more explosive, and more coordinated, the bar should be raised to challenge them to keep getting better. Our parents, coaches, bosses, managers, or leaders set standards so we can, hopefully, always reflect the best and most productive versions of ourselves.

Yet, as we start to mature and develop, we can form our own standards. For example, many people develop standards for who they want to date. "He needs to be 6 feet tall, bald, have a goatee, no kids, good job, homeowner, and debt-free." Or, "She has to be sporty, smart, not too sassy, no kids, built like Kim Kardashian, and have a good job." These are all shallow standards, in my opinion. Notice the failure to mention how they would like to be treated or the character they'd like their ideal partner to possess?

Some people create standards for how they want to be treated, while others develop standards for the type of job they'd like to have.

As such, this chapter will help you set standards for essential parts of your life: relationships, how you want to be treated, career path, etc.

IT'S UP TO YOU TO TEACH PEOPLE WHAT YOUR STANDARDS ARE

As a personal trainer at Nike World Headquarters, I had a very outspoken client. She would be funny one day and then mean-spirited the next. Depending on how her day was going in her job at Nike, she let that feeling dominate our 60-minute workout session. During one particular session, I could tell she was having a pretty horrible day. She was fifteen minutes late, and as I stood at the top of the stairs waiting for her to go and change, I thought about how I could make this training session the highlight of her day.

Should I take her outside so she could enjoy the sunshine, or should I challenge her with some strength and stability work in our state-of-the-art weight room? Ahh, I will do both! She came up the stairs and said not one word to me. As we entered the strength training part of the session, she began calling me Alexandra. She said, matter-of-factly, "Alexandra — I like that name for you." I replied, "What gives you the impression that I am okay with being called Alexandra?" She got quiet. She ignored me again. I engaged her in a running circuit outside, during which I thought about what to say to her.

She finished, and while she walked towards me, I said, "I know you most likely had a rough time at work today, but I refuse to be a punching bag for anyone. If you don't like your job or if it's affecting you emotionally, then quit or figure out how you can deal with it." When I had first started this conversation, I made it a point not to let the emotion of anger take over. I know what that looks and feels like because I dealt with it growing up in a house with alcoholic parents who often physically fought with one another. That same emotion served me well when I played football, but only because it was focused on aggression.

I continued, "I refuse to be called out of my name, and it's up to me to let you know that I will not tolerate this. I'm okay with you being mad at me because my standards allow me to be okay with *you* not liking me rather than *me* not liking me."

She sent me an email later on that day, profusely

apologizing and explaining why she had acted the way she did. If I had never told her my standards, she would have most likely continued acting this way whenever she had a bad day at work.

It's up to you to set the standards for how you want to be treated. Don't assume people will treat you nicely or reasonably, even if they're paying you or vice versa.

HOW TO DEVELOP YOUR OWN STANDARDS

Personal standards are a set of behaviors we consistently act upon. If you have high standards, your behaviors will elevate per your specific goals. If you have low standards, you will most likely have low self-esteem that opens you up to negative influences or being taken advantage of. The good thing is that you can decide how to set your own standards. Your parents played a huge role in doing so — good or bad — but you can make adjustments accordingly, deciding if you are a person with low or high standards.

You are constantly sending signals out to the world about who you are: how you dress, how you act, how you handle finances, how you view your health, and the promises you keep. All of these things broadcast your standards.

Depending on the clothes you wear, the cleanliness of your appearance, and how you talk and walk, someone can and most likely will create a story in their minds about who you are. Others can hypothesize what type of standards you have. If they think you have low personal standards, they will judge and modify their thoughts and interactions accordingly. But if they deem you to have high standards, they are more likely to show you respect. If they respect you and consistently display high-character traits, you will be more likely to win their admiration. With admiration comes influence.

When developing high standards for your life, start with self-love. You can begin the process with daily affirmations. Look in the mirror and repeat to yourself, "I love you," "You are worth it," or even "You are a certified BEAST"; this can spark something within you. I used to perform this exercise before every football game—even in high school. It didn't matter if I had played lousy the previous game or was facing a future Hall of Famer; I would constantly acknowledge my self-love and stature as a certified beast.

The next step is to model the behavior of others in whom you see high standards. If it's not your parents, that's perfectly fine. Use the person who you know beyond a shadow of a doubt has high standards as the inspiration to set the same for yourself.

The person I modeled my health standard after was Ron Brown. Ron was the gym supervisor at the Tutt Unit Boys Club in Colorado Springs. From 5th grade to 9th grade during the school year, I went to the Boys Club after school until 7 p.m. During the summer months, my brother and I would spend the entire day there from 9 a.m. until 5 p.m., Monday through Friday.

After checking in at the front desk, I would run down to the gym to say hello to Ron. I would watch him like a hawk. He was 6'3" and about 245 pounds of "twisted steel," as he used to say. He would shoot free throws, coach kids to play different basketball games, and work on his mobility exercises and stretches every day. One day, he invited me to lift weights with him. I couldn't say yes fast enough. He showed me the proper form for each exercise: squat, lunge, pull-up, barbell row, even a plank. Ron showed me exactly how to do each one and why it is so important to strengthen your body if you want to play sports.

"Alex," he would say, "Your body is your temple. You need to fortify it with a strong foundation." I remember those words like it was yesterday. Ron inspired me to create a standard for health and physical fitness.

- Who can inspire *you* to set new standards in your life?

- Do you know them and their character?

- Which of your goals will require you to develop new and higher standards?

In the previous chapter, "Assessment," I spoke about the importance of assessing your current reality. You must be intentional in the varied roles you play in your life, asking yourself if associated standards are okay, low, or too high. From the goals that you set, you should be able to quickly answer these questions. More challenging questions you need to ask yourself are:

- Are the standards yours, or were they placed on you?

- When did you create these standards? Have you outgrown them?

- Do they still align with your vision of your future self?

NEVER COMPARE YOURSELF WITH OTHERS

As you start to create new standards for the different facets of your life, it's essential to take small incremental steps to create new daily rituals, which will soon become habits. If you stay consistent, these habits will become a part of you and lead you to new and better decisions, reactions, and actions.

The rituals must help you plan and prepare you for a better version of yourself. Growth is the goal, and raising your standards is the best way to grow yourself. When you raise your standards, you must be aware that most people are okay with being average. Social norms will tell you to lower your standards.

Many people do the bare minimum to stay in shape, learn a new language, or even prepare for a sporting event. They will often compare themselves to others, but you must avoid doing this when trying to make it to your next level. The only person you should compare yourself to is *you*. When you compare yourself with others, you subconsciously lower your standards because most people are unwilling to work on themselves or sacrifice time and energy to grow. It is so important to monitor yourself in the areas you want to improve in. Weight loss, fitness, athleticism, finances, knowledge, memory, and decision-making: All these things help show who you are, and you must keep track of them to see your growth or lack of development.

Before my rookie year, my agent connected me with Raymond Farris, a trainer in the San Francisco Bay Area. Raymond had trained a bunch of professional athletes in the area: Barry Bonds, Ricky Watters, Steve Bono, J.J. Stokes, and Dana Stubblefield were just a few of his clients. But the one person who influenced me the most, despite saying the fewest number of words to me, was Jerry Rice.

Jerry would show up to our workouts at least 20 minutes early to do his prep before our actual warm-up. Everything he did was at 100 percent. Jerry's cone drills for foot quickness, 10-yard get-offs, 40-yard speed build-ups, 1-on-1 drills, and even his cool down seemed to be at game speed. I often thought to myself, "If this is the speed that Jerry works out or practices, how much faster, quicker, and more focused is he in games?"

Our field sessions would last 2 hours, and then we would spend about an hour doing our strength training. I would watch Jerry closely: how much weight he lifted, how long it took him to get fatigued, how perfect or imperfect his form was. Sometimes, I'd even count his reps while I was counting mine! It was exhausting.We would train like this Monday through Friday.

On Fridays, we would go and run "The Hill," 2.5 miles of pain and suffering. It was a narrow path with branches and occasional creeks that ran alongside it. It was somewhat flat at some points, but most of it was uphill. As we prepared to run, Raymond quietly told me, "Jerry does this in under 19 minutes." I didn't know why he said that to me in that moment.

My time was 23 minutes, 22 seconds. My legs trembled as I walked to the parking lot after that horrific leg and lung workout. It took me about 10 minutes to even start up my car. While waiting, I figured out why Raymond shared Jerry's time: He wanted me to know the standard set by the very best.

After working with and against Jerry for three months, I had built up enough credibility with respect to work ethic. After one of our field sessions, while switching out of our cleats to prepare to drive to the gym, Jerry said, "Hey young fella, you want some advice?" My mind was doing cartwheels. "Sure," I said. "Never compare your standards with someone else's standards, and don't be afraid to raise the bar." I asked, "Raise the bar?" He continued, "When you continually meet your standards and you don't raise the bar, complacency can set in. Don't ever be complacent." Those words were like gold to me and have helped in so many areas of my life.

Jerry knew that Raymond would often compare his time on the hill run or even his work ethic with the other guys. If you couldn't beat his time, it would cause resentment towards the hill, Jerry, or even Raymond. I think that's why Jerry shared that advice with me that day. He didn't want me to resent him in my fruitless quest to meet his standards; because after all, he is the GOAT, and he knew it!

On the flip side, if Jerry's standard was achievable for me or any other athlete, we could have possibly assumed we'd made it and didn't have to work as hard anymore. That's why it is so important to continually raise the "bar" for your standards.

HIGH ACHIEVER NUGGETS:

- In what parts of your life do you need to raise the bar (relationships, career, character, etc.)?

- Are there areas in your life where the bar is too high?- What tells you that the bar is too high?

- Do you compare specific parts of your life to someone else's experience? Why? Does social media play a role in this? Remember, people often only share the highlights, not their reality.

CHAPTER 13:

THE COMMITMENT CONNUNDRUM:

The Transfer Portal Paradox

— ◇ —

In one of the mentorship programs that I do for college sports programs, one of the athletes asked me a viral question. That question pertained to transferring. I said to him,

"Why would you want to transfer Champ?"

He replied, "Man, the coach told me I would get a fair shot,"

I said, "Wait, you've been here all of four months," he was a freshman early admit. "You have to do a couple of things, my man. First, you need to understand that nothing in this world is given. It is earned." I continued, "So what... you're third string at the beginning of spring football! After my redshirt year, I came into spring football training camp fourth string. I'm not going to lie; I was butt-hurt. But I quickly got out of my feelings and looked at the job at hand.

I needed to figure out what the guys in front of me weren't doing and adjust my game accordingly. I also figured out that I needed to do the extra work (before and after practice) with my techniques and turning my weaknesses into strengths. Because of this game plan that I executed, four weeks later I was named the starter, and the rest is history."

He looked at me and nodded his head in agreement.

I continued, "the second thing you need to do is get out of your feelings!" He looked at me with an uncomfortable smile. I said, "some of the worst decisions people make in life are made based on how they feel, not based on data, facts, experience, knowledge, ability, or even their relationships." I reflected briefly, "Just think if I would have transferred after being fourth in the depth chart. I wouldn't have been a part of history. I most likely wouldn't have had the opportunity to play in the Rose Bowl. I probably wouldn't have been a first-round draft pick. I wouldn't have met my wife and had eight beautiful kids, and I definitely wouldn't be in front of you right now."

He said, "Wow! I didn't think this deep about making a big decision like this."

I told him, "Most kids don't because they feel their way through situations and relationships instead of thinking about the positive and negative ramifications of their decisions."

The ability to overcome challenges is a valuable asset no matter what the environment is. Sooner or later, you will have to answer why you avoided different adversities in your life. Your actions, not your words, tell people who you are. It also is a considerable component of predicting behavior.

I remember watching, from afar, this superstar high school quarterback. He was a coveted 4-star recruit who had major colleges drooling over him. He committed and de-committed to 3 different schools before finally accepting a scholarship to a school whose football program was consistently ranked in the top 10 in all the major poles. Once he got there, he realized the level of competition, the attention to detail, and the commitment that it would take to crack the starting lineup. He fought hard to develop himself physically, but he found it hard to get on the field. After three years, he transferred to another big-time school. It was still hard for him to get consistent, quality reps on the field. After 1.5 years, he moved yet again, but to a smaller FCS school. The jury is still out on him being able to play quality football at the collegiate level.

I see this a lot with athletes in general.

But let's look a bit deeper.

Future employers, professional sports teams, and any other industry are just like coaches. They will look at "your tape," aka (your resume) to try to get a sense of who you are. If you have the propensity to leave a team or job every year or two, at some point, you will have to answer the question of "why." Make no mistake about it; people will have already done their homework on you.

There is something to be said about going through adversity, having patience, and overcoming the odds no matter what you have committed to.

Commitment is a huge foundational component that makes people very successful. If you fall out of love with something or somebody, if you are being mistreated in any form or fashion, if you are not getting joy out of something that used to give you a large amount of it, I have to ask you a question. How do you define love, fairness, and joy? I also have to ask this final question, is it worth fighting for? I would suggest keeping your commitments unless they are toxic or become toxic. If the commitment is bringing out the worst in you therefore, it's not helping you become the best version of yourself, or it is hurting you or others, I would say it is time to leave that situation or commitment.

CHAPTER 14:

RECAP

— ◇ —

When I played ball, I learned an important lesson from coach Willie Shaw. He would tell us how important it was to take notes before, during, and after watching film. He would preach to us about how "real professionals" always help themselves out by recapping a practice or game.

"When you do a recap, it just sticks," he would say. I would take out my notepad (one might use an iPhone nowadays) and jot down a recap of the key points I learned about myself, our opponent, the scheme, personnel, etc. This type of strategic planning helped me find success as a student-athlete and professional athlete. I took that valuable skill with me when transitioning into my career as a personal trainer, consultant, and now, speaker. I would recap every training session, phone call, meeting, or presentation. I would write down or leave myself an audio recording of what I (or the other person) would commit to, as well as other pertinent information. I found that having those notes was invaluable for my success. So, as we approach the end of this book, let me provide a quick recap to ensure you gain the most value out of this resource.

Key 1: Understand Leadership

Understanding and using leadership to make better decisions and get what you want out of any situation is the biggest key. But first, we must define leadership, which when boiled down, is influence.

- Character – who you are

- Ability – what you are capable of

- Knowledge – what you know

- Success – what you have achieved

- Failure – what you failed to achieve

- Platform – what you do

- Experience – where you have been

- Intuition – how you feel

- Communication – how you share

- Relationships – who you know

When you understand each aspect of these influencers, you will not only see changes in yourself with respect to self-awareness, but also in how you see these influencers work in friends, teammates, coaches, bosses, and managers: basically, people who are or could be influential in your life.

Key 2: Alignment

How do you align with your foundation? Is it your family,

friends, faith, hobbies, material objects? You should be able to rank these in order. What would happen if your health were to fail or you break up with your boyfriend/girlfriend or go bankrupt? Would you still be able to move forward, attacking your life's goals or mission? You must be firmly aligned with your foundation.

Key 3: Assignment

Finding your purpose is something that can be placed on your shoulders from an early age (à la Tiger Woods) or require some deep personal self-awareness work, which takes time. I would work to find your life's assignment on your own or with the help of a mentor or personal development coach. That person should ask you questions that stir up emotions that are potentially stronger than those you ever had when competing in your sport. Understanding who you are is your foundation. Finding your purpose is the seed. Adjustment is the action that is required.

Key 4: Adjustment

What type of character will allow you to adjust to find the type of career, relationships, and environments that will bring joy to your life? This will require thinking ahead, but if you want to use the platform of sports to get you where you want to go in life, you'll have to adjust how people see you. You are more than an athlete, and it is *your* job to convince people of this.

An easy way to do so is through social media. Your posts, how you comment, and who you follow or share comments about all create an image of who you are. Be mindful of this and use it to create your ideal personal narrative.

Key 5: Assessment

Watching film to learn if we hit our goals for the game is mandatory to find success. If you want to improve in anything, you must find a way to measure it. *Feeling* that you're getting better is way different than *knowing*: facts over feelings.

Set weekly themed goals towards what you want to achieve (connecting with people, reading, working on a strategy to understand you and the character you want to have, etc.).

- We do this to know if we're improving or falling backward. You never stay the same. Every day, you either get better or worse.

- Ask others if they have seen a change in you, as your desire to change for the better might not show through. Do your actions, behaviors, and words reflect a positive change?

- Are you asking better questions? Are you making better decisions? Are you getting better results on a consistent basis?

Key 6: No Plan B

Committing to the journey and removing the "safety net(s)" in your life can force you to become more creative and resilient. These same foundational principles can help you in life outside of your sport.

When you are laser-focused on who you want to be and what you want to do, it's time to put together a game plan to get there.

What do you need to have in place in the absence of a plan B?

- Know what you're trying to do or achieve

- Recognize the negatives, not just the positives

- Ensure resources are available

- Practice who you are on the daily:

o Know that habits will lay the foundation

o Employ the same habits that helped you in your sport (waking up early, staying late, working hard on your weaknesses, etc.)

o Get it done: do whatever you need to do to reach your goals and dreams, even if that means suffering a few losses along the wayo Rely on the same principles you used when first starting in your sport (e.g., professional baseball players didn't hit home runs in the pee wee leagues)

o Develop a "burn the ships" mentality

Key #7: Recognize the Power of Environments

Making changes to your environment makes it easier to do what's right without the need to think about staying motivated. If you construct your environment so that making sound decisions comes easily, you can set yourself up to practice better habits.

Often, we think that change comes from within. We believe that achieving a goal is about adjusting ourselves and what we think. Yet, we discount the fact that optimizing our environment to make better choices can have a large impact on our actions. Keeping a better option within reach makes it the default choice.

Key #8: Develop Your Procedures and Protocols

Learning the fundamentals of your sport, weightlifting, or working on a class project is not about grasping the basics; it's about learning and processing the essential elements of those things. Fundamentals are not basic factors you can just toss aside; rather, they are essential to find success. If you lack the fundamentals, you lack a solid foundation and are susceptible to injury, setbacks, and wasted time and energy. If you are a young athlete, you can develop your own procedures and protocols based on what you want to achieve during and after college. I suggest asking yourself these questions:

- Who would you impact (other than yourself) if you didn't follow procedures and protocols in and out of your sport?

- What freedoms would you sacrifice in order to enjoy short-term pleasure?

- What type of discipline would you need to graduate? Is this the same or different from when you're playing your sport?

Regardless of success or failure, stick with a proven procedure. Be patient, believe in the system, and let success come to you. Don't chase it!

Key #9: Create a Relationship Roadmap

How do you approach building relationships with others? First, you need to connect with yourself. Learn your passions, skills, and opportunities for growth. Get to know people for the sake of doing so. You may learn something about an individual you might not like and choose not to associate with that person to avoid adverse effects on you and your brand.

Most importantly, look to add value when meeting new people. This may take shape as a simple conversation or even an ask to serve (such as a free internship). If you are a student-athlete, this role provides opportunities to meet people at all different levels. Be strategic when connecting with people who can affect your growth; that starts with being upfront with them. Nobody likes a con artist.

Key #10: Use Adversity as an Advantage

The same things that can provide an advantage can also become a disadvantage. Growing up with privileges like enjoying a great home life, access to resources like athletic training and coaching, great teachers, and wonderful schools can lead you to take these things for granted.

Athletes are notorious for possessing the ability to block out distractions when in stressful environments. Yet, they are also known for having tunnel vision, leading them to miss key reasons why they got the results they did. Examining your situation from different angles can allow you to see that adversity was perhaps a key component of your success.

Growing up in an environment without resources—like knowing the lights might be turned off because your mom couldn't pay the electric bill, scarce food options, a lack of parental love/guidance, or even the possibility of abuse in the home—can harden you and make you more resilient. Those disadvantages can be a huge advantage, but it all depends on the character of the person enduring these situations.

Your character can either spiral you into the depths of anger, self-hate, abuse, and suffering, or push you toward people and places you've only dreamed of. It can also shape how you view the world; but it is a choice! How do *you* want to employ any adversity nuggets in your life?

Your environment can shape you, but you get to decide if it will do so positively or negatively.

Key #11: Evolving Your Standards

A standard is different than a rule. A standard dictates what you do, and you act accordingly. Consider a bar for a high jumper. It can be raised or lowered depending on ability, and as high jumpers get stronger, more explosive, and more coordinated, the bar should be raised to challenge them to keep getting better. Our parents, coaches, bosses, managers, or leaders set standards so we can, hopefully, always reflect the best and most productive versions of ourselves.

Personal standards are a set of behaviors we consistently act upon. If you have high standards, your behaviors will elevate according to your specific goals. If you have low standards, you will most likely have low self-esteem, opening you up to negative influences or being taken advantage of.

It's up to you to teach people what your standards are. Don't assume everyone else's are the same as yours. Never compare yourself with others, which may cause you to resent yourself or them.

Closing Comments

For all you student-athletes out there, I totally get it! The complexities of this role are tough. But make sure you understand: Nobody will care about this when you seek out a job or career. Employers want to see and hear about how you made the best use of your time and energy.

How can you articulate the sacrifices you made? What did your experience teach you? How did you overcome adversity despite all the pressure that usually accompanies elite-level athletics?

You have it in you! When I say "it," I mean the things that set you apart from other people: hard work, focus, accountability, mental strength, time management skills, communication, ability to take feedback, teamwork, team building, and relationship building. All these things can impact you as you enter the business world, the educational world, the health care world, or the entrepreneurial world.

Understanding who you are and what you want to achieve is a good place to start. But possessing the capacity to lead yourself and others is what will drive you to have the impact desired in any given arena. You can't wait for it to happen to you: You have to go and take it. Use the resources and relationships in front of you, and don't be afraid to ask for help. Investing in yourself is the biggest and most important thing you can do to become the best version of yourself!

HIGH ACHIEVER COACHING POINTS:

- How will you leverage your experience as an athlete?

- What character is needed for you to become the best

version of yourself?-Who can help if you struggle when transitioning into the real world?

- What will you do with your life?

FROM THE HEART

My wife and I have always preached to our kids that no matter how good of an athlete you are, you must understand who you are because you are more than just sports. Everybody else will see them as athletes, but when that platform is gone, I don't want them to feel the way I did when my football career was over (not knowing my purpose or calling in life). That is the primary thing we want our kids to understand. First, when working on yourself, learn what you like and don't like (engage in many new activities, things you never thought about trying or doing: golf, skydiving, bowling, sales, building, etc.). Don't be afraid to take on jobs or roles in varied fields. Take advantage of your youth: It's the perfect time to experiment with different career ideas and paths, but you must first understand and own who you are. Second, make every attempt to discover your passion outside of your sport. Third, your character will always outlast your athleticism, looks, knowledge, or even experience. Treat people with respect no matter where they are in life, and remember the "Golden Rule": Treat others how you want to be treated. Love & Respect.

ABOUT THE AUTHOR

You have climbed to the top of the mountain. You are an athlete who has done some phenomenal things. You know what it takes to lead and win. But what do you do when it's time to transition out of the sports arena (or off the field) and join the "real world?" So much of what you've done on your platform was cheered and sometimes jeered. Your character has been intertwined with your athletic ability since you were a kid, and once you exit(ed) your sport, you find yourself lost.

This is where I come in. I work with athletes, celebrities, entrepreneurs, and Fortune 500 executives to align their purpose with their passion, assigning whom they want to become and where they want to go. I then help uncover beneficial character and relationship adjustments so they can live their life to the fullest.

I love spending time with my wife and our eight children playing some hoop, golfing, and smashing them in table tennis, foosball or dominoes.

Are you ready to have more influence in your life and the lives of others? It's simple! Feel free to reach out to me through any channel mentioned below, and let's get a call scheduled.

Connect with Me

https://www.facebook.com/alexmolden1

https://www.facebook.com/groups/417456045552437

https://twitter.com/alexmolden

https://www.linkedin.com/in/alex-molden-9693431b/

https://www.instagram.com/alexmolden/?hl=en

https://alexmoldenspeaks.com/

info@alexmoldenspeaks.com

Made in the USA
Coppell, TX
27 July 2022

80530958R00085